CHASE!

MANAGING YOUR DOG'S PREDATORY INSTINCTS

CLARISSA VON REINHARDT

Dogwise™ Publishing

Wenatchee, Washington U.S.A.

Chase!
Managing Your Dog's Predatory Instincts
Clarissa von Reinhardt

Dogwise Publishing
A Division of Direct Book Service, Inc.
403 South Mission Street, Wenatchee, Washington 98801
1-509-663-9115, 1-800-776-2665
www.dogwisepublishing.com / info@dogwisepublishing.com

Originally published in Germany under the title Das unerwünschte Jagdverhalten des Hundes © 2005

Photographs: Annette Gevatter, Anja Birke-Haardt, Ulrike Hasenmeier-Reimer, Anne Lill Kvam, Birgit Neumark, Gudrun Hundertmark, Konrad Dolderer, M. Rohlf, istockphoto
Illustrations: Jürgen Zimmermann, Stuttgart
Graphic Design: Lindsay Peternell

ISBN: 978-1-929242-68-9

Library of Congress Cataloging-in-Publication Data
Reinhardt, Clarissa von.
  [Unerwunschte Jagdverhalten des Hundes. English]
  Chase! : managing your dog's predatory instincts / Clarissa von Reinhardt.
     p. cm.
  ISBN 978-1-929242-68-9
  1. Dogs--Training. 2. Dogs--Behavior. 3. Predatory animals--Psychology.
     I. Title.
  SF431.R42613 2010
  636.7'0835--dc22
                        2010005276

Printed in the U.S.A.

Contents

Introduction 1

1. Predatory Behavior 3

2. Foundation Training 21

3. Communicative Walks as Key to Training Success 36

4. Behaviors to Master 48

5. Play and Other Activities 77

6. Training Methods and Their Limits 95

Postscript: The Story of Fenargi 116

Closing Thoughts 119

Thanks 121

Further Reading 122

Index 123

About the Author 128

More praise for *Chase!*

A great read for anyone who has struggled to come to grips with a dog who chases other animals. *Chase!* provides a comprehensive training program that addresses both the mental and physical needs of these challenging dogs and resoundingly refutes the need for aversive techniques. The training program is one that many dogs would raise their paws to, whether they have a high predatory instinct or not.

Terry Long, CPDT-KA, editor of the *APDT Chronicle of the Dog's* "On Behavior" column and author of *The Whole Dog Journal's* "Good Sports" series

Understanding a dog's predatory nature can take years. The ability to help teach a novice handler to help their dogs step by step is a real gift. Clarissa has written a wonderful book on how to humanly and successfully work with our canine friends. She is clear it will take time and patience and to not hurry the process. This is one of the best books you can read to help guardians and their prey driven dogs help one another successfully become a team—and to strengthen the bond between them. You will learn to communicate openly and find joy and solace enjoying the countryside without the worry of the dog chasing wild game or cats. Congratulations Clarissa...

Dee Ganley, CPDT, CABC, CAP2, Author of *Changing People Changing Dogs, Positive Solutions for Working with Dogs*

Introduction

Dogs who have a strong desire to chase things—deer, squirrels, cars, bicyclists, running children, etc.—present their owners many frustrating problems. A dog who suddenly takes off running after whatever he perceives to be "prey" can cause all sorts of difficulties and become a danger to himself, you, and whoever or whatever he is chasing. The reaction of most owners who face this situation is to try to stop the behavior by such means as keeping the dog tightly on-leash at all times, resorting to the use of shock collars and electronic fences, or even having the dog chained up for hours on end. There are people who are more than happy to try to sell you on a "quick and easy" solution, but most are ineffective or inhumane. As you will learn in this book, you can use positive training methods to help manage this problem.

The predatory dive your dog may be displaying is both complex and fascinating, and it is important that you understand it in order to keep it under control. Predatory behaviors in dogs are:

- Both hereditary and shaped during early development.
- Are natural instincts aroused by the environment.
- Learned in part by imitation.
- Influenced by the actions of others.
- Frequently, though not always, linked to hunger.
- Need to be practiced.
- May depend on the dog's individual nature and preferences.

Although it is obvious that we cannot allow our pet dogs free rein to always live out this behavior in the modern world, I find the capabilities they come equipped with fascinating. Their olfactory abilities are legendary, but they also utilize other senses to locate prey. In a flash, a strategy is developed and followed, sometimes culminating in the desired result—at least from the dog's point of view! This drive may be so strong that even if the prey does manage to escape, the dog will not give up.

If you want to create a suitable training plan to prevent troublesome prey behavior from developing in your dog, you must first understand how this behavior has evolved. In order to apply effective intervention at the right moment, you need to know about the behavior of the canid in great detail—its character, the role of predation, the use of its senses, its body language, how it manifests itself in different types of breeds, and much more.

Intervening to control this behavior must never involve violence toward or pain for the dog. The question of the effectiveness or non-effectiveness of aversive training methods (which I examine in Chapter 6) is of secondary importance. First and foremost, it is a question of fairness and morality. I am completely convinced that we have no right to punish an animal for an instinctive behavior that has been genetically determined through a long evolutionary process.

I have chosen to focus largely on chase and prey behavior that dogs exhibit toward other animals. The rural part of Germany in which I live has extensive forests, game parks, and parklands. Dogs chasing and harming other animals is a very common problem. In more urbanized areas, of course, dogs may exhibit chase and prey behavior toward running children, cars, bicyclists, squirrels, ducks, etc. The techniques and training methods I recommend apply in either circumstance. However, if your dog is exhibiting a prey drive toward people or moving vehicles, the consequences to both the dog and its intended "victim" can be very serious. In this case, I would recommend that you seek the help and advice of a professional trainer. At the very least, be very careful working with your dog in an area where, if you lose control of him, he runs a risk of harming someone, something, or himself.

This book is my invitation to you to delve into this fascinating and complex behavior which often manifests itself in domestic dogs, and to discover a training program that completely rejects the use of aversive stimuli. This program will strengthen the bond between you and your dog and can be a lot of fun for both of you as well.

CHAPTER 1
PREDATORY BEHAVIOR

Predation is influenced by a whole host of behavioral patterns, many of which are genetically determined and others that are shaped by the environment in which a dog lives. The ancestors of the modern dog were both hunters and scavengers. Obviously, dogs in the wild who showed skill in locating, hunting, and killing prey survived and passed these traits on to their offspring. These predatory traits remain in the modern domestic dog, although more so in some dogs than in others.

Predatory behavior patterns

In general, chase and prey behaviors occur when the dog becomes aware of stimuli that trigger whatever predatory drive the dog possesses. These triggers almost always involve movement, such as a butterfly in flight, a jumping rabbit, a jogger running past, or even just a piece of paper blowing about in the wind. Most of these things are largely uninteresting to and therefore ignored by the dog once they stop moving, do not run away or run around, and so on. However, if they do continue to move, the dog may react instinctively by chasing and trying to catch them.

Behavioral patterns related to predation, which can take on a more serious character at a later stage, are often playfully experimented with and perfected during the puppy phase—even as early as the sixth week of life! These include:

- Stalking.
- Intense staring (eye stalking).
- The "attack."
- The grab-bite.
- Carrying away and guarding prey.

A young dog displaying stalking and staring behaviors.

A young dog doesn't learn these behaviors through self-directed experimentation alone, but also by imitating the actions he sees performed by his mother or other adult dogs. For this reason, you should take great care (especially in the puppy and young dog phases) that an older dog does not show your dog where "the rabbit runs"—in the truest sense of the term. While your dog may not have indicated any interest in chasing prey, even when they run right past his nose, you should not underestimate the danger of mood transfer from another dog. If there is another dog nearby who races off, barking loudly, the chances are that your dog will run after him. If this isn't the case, I hope you can appreciate how really lucky you are.

A puppy seeks, finds, and kills prey.

When young canines in the wild are around four weeks old, the mother dog begins to demonstrate behavioral patterns to them. For example, lying down in front of the pups with a bone and gnawing on it demonstrably. Then she might bring her puppies dead prey animals—or large chunks of them—on which they can practice the best way to use their paws and fangs for holding and eating. Later, the mother will bring them live prey animals (that are capable of attempting to flee) in order to provide the puppies with training material. From our perspective, this may seem gruesome, but it is of enormous importance for survival in the wild.

Over time puppies learn—slowly but surely—the skills they need to survive by imitating others. Through trial and error (another learning principle), they discover the best way to gnaw a bone, and then to catch, hold, and also kill prey. A wild dog or wolf who doesn't learn these skills will not be able to survive.

Stalking prey is also learned by imitation. In the wild, when the puppies are juveniles, they accompany older dogs on the hunt. Once more, they learn by first watching and then imitating, through experimenting and perfecting—and each time they get better at it. Of course, individual talent also plays a role, not only in the wild, but also with domesticated dogs. While one dog may be very good at persistently following a scent or capturing prey, another may be less talented. A hunter would be delighted to have the former, a dog owner with no interest in hunting, the latter.

A modern pack

A few years ago, some clients came to me with an adopted dog with an unusual history. Until the dog was six months old, he had lived and also hunted (successfully, I must add) in a real pack with his parents and siblings. The entire dog family would disappear for hours or days into the depths of the Bavarian forest and come back home smeared in blood and satisfied, their bellies full. Their former owners found it simply enthralling that their dogs engaged in real pack behavior and gave them complete freedom to do so. Of course, the forays by the dogs into the forest didn't go unnoticed, and there were serious problems with hunters who threatened to shoot the dogs. When it became clear the owners were not going to come to their senses, the county vet ordered all of the dogs to be impounded. They were brought to an animal shelter and then placed in new homes.

Unfortunately, when clients of mine adopted one of these dogs, they were not informed of the highly developed predatory behavior they would have to deal with. It was, to put it mildly, a disaster. Overall, the dog was very nice, friendly, and great with people because, despite his forays into the forest, he had been in contact with people from a young age. In urban areas he was easy to walk on-leash and obeyed simple commands, even when highly distracted—as long as the distraction didn't involve prey. When he got into the countryside in a forested area, you could forget obedience and walking him successfully. He tracked the entire time and became alert at the slightest snap in the underbrush. If he saw even the smallest of animals—such as a squirrel—you could no longer communicate with him. He yelped and howled, then leaped with his full 88-pound weight to the end of his leash, stood on his hind legs like a horse, and went absolutely wild. He is now ten years of age and gradually getting calmer. However, taking him for walks is still not an easy task, despite a lot of training.

The predatory sequence

Predatory behavior consists of an entire sequence of behavioral patterns. First, the prey must be located, which can take a few minutes, hours, or even days. This is dependent on the extent of the hunting area, the size of the potential prey animal population, the season, the weather, and many other factors. If the prey is in the immediate vicinity, the orientation posture (for example, some dogs "point") is assumed until the animal is actually sighted. Next comes stalking and, should the dog be in a pack with others, encircling in preparation for downing large prey. Finally, the part of the sequence that requires the highest amount of energy takes place—chasing the prey until it is caught, then attacking, grabbing, and finally killing it. The prey is then dissected and consumed. If the prey is big enough, pieces of it will be taken away and buried for later consumption.

This entire sequence can, under certain circumstances, take a long time. In winter, a hunting strategy for wolves might include driving a large prey animal, such as an elk or bison, into the water and not letting it out for hours or days on end until the animal is so cold and exhausted that it can hardly defend itself when it is attacked.

Overview of the predatory sequence

- Finding the prey
- Orientation posture
- Sighting the prey
- Stalking/encircling
- Chasing/driving
- Attacking (grabbing)
- Killing
- Dissecting
- Consuming and/or carrying away and burying (storing).

Pointing, an orientation posture display.

Killing and killing strategies

There are a number of strategies dog or wolves may use for killing a prey animal. What is chosen usually depends upon the size of the prey.

Small prey animals such as mice, moles, etc., are killed by the so-called "mouse pounce." The dog or wolf jumps on the prey animal with such force that it normally breaks the prey's neck or spine. Then it is held with the front paws, secured in the dog's or wolf's fangs, and eaten.

Mid-size prey animals such as rabbits are grabbed by the neck from above and shaken. Again, death occurs through breaking the animal's neck.

Large prey animals such as elk or deer can be killed only through cooperative hunting by the pack. The capabilities needed to do this are only partially found in today's domestic dogs, although it is sometimes amazing with what precision several dogs suddenly and instinctively form a left and right flank, encircle a prey animal, make eye contact, and attack simultaneously. While sometimes they manage to get this far, they may lack the experience to grab and kill the prey.

Different strategies are adopted depending on the size of prey.

I have often heard reports about a dog chasing a deer, a rabbit, or the neighbor's hamster, only to end up not knowing what to do with it once he cornered it. However, you can't rely on that happening. Even if you are confident your dog will not harm the prey animal, understand that the prey "victim" is subjected to an enormous amount of stress and thus chasing should not be permitted if you can avoid it. From an animal welfare standpoint, I am annoyed when someone allows their dog to chase after a deer, rabbit, or cat and tries to play it down by saying, "He won't catch it anyway."

A self-rewarding action

The act of chasing prey constitutes what is termed a self-rewarding action. Whether the prey is caught or not, chasing proves very reinforcing for many dogs, probably like what a human experiences during what is called an "adrenaline high." It can be so self-rewarding that you will never be able to control your dog's behavior if you constantly permit him to chase after prey, even when the situation doesn't seem dangerous. If you do allow it, you may not be able to stop him when there's a hunter nearby or a busy road lies between the dog and the prey. The release of adrenaline during the chase ensures that the chase itself is self-rewarding for the dog even if the prey is not caught.

For this reason, "hunting" can occur even when a dog is not hungry. While a dog who is really hungry is more likely to search for prey than one who is lying in the sun with a full belly, you nevertheless may see well nourished, recently fed dogs ecstatically pursuing prey simply because the chase itself gives them that "kick."

Breed disposition

It is beyond the scope of this book to present information on every breed and its tendency to engage in predatory behavior. However, I would like to quickly summarize a few points which will help you correctly assess your breed and to be prepared accordingly. First, I recommend doing some research into the breed of the dog you own or are thinking about getting. Ask the breeder a lot of questions because they frequently tend to extol only the "good" points of the breed and say nothing about, or simply play down, the disadvantages. While there are breeders who will give you complete and accurate information, unfortunately they are not in the majority. So go beyond just relying on a breeder and undertake some additional research in books and on the internet. Above all, take the time to talk to people who live with such a dog. It may also be a good idea to ask your vet about his experience because, through over-breeding, many breeds have a tendency for certain diseases and illnesses. The more you know, the better.

All dogs can be interested in prey, but in some breeds specific elements of predatory behavior have been selected for and accentuated through breeding. For example: retrieving in retrievers; pointing in pointers; stalking, encircling, and driving in herding dogs.

A Golden Retriever doing what he is bred for—retrieving.

Prey aggression was also cultivated in terriers. The idea was to breed dogs who were small and agile and would fearlessly pursue prey, especially rats. By far the most noteworthy are the hunting terriers, but other types of terriers have astonishing potential that owners do not always know how to handle. The West Highland Terrier and the Jack Russell Terrier, for example, are popular family dogs and can be found everywhere, especially in cities. Despite their cute looks and agreeable size, these terriers may constantly upset the entire neighborhood by standing at the garden fence and barking, chasing cats up a tree, or defending a freshly killed mouse against everything and everyone. Owners are often surprised because they do not understand their dog's drives.

Then there are breeds that exhibit a very strong desire to run. These breeds include not only sled dogs (such as Huskies),

In Border Collies, crouching, stalking, and driving have each been selected through breeding.

Lest we forget: even these terriers were originally bred—(and still possess a lot of talent)—for hunting.

and sight hounds (such as Greyhounds and Borzois), but also most hunting dogs including retrievers, setters, pointers, and many others. Some of these breeds are sprinters who can reach high speeds for short stretches, while others are long distance endurance runners. A sprinter can move hundreds of yards away from you in a matter of several seconds.

If you do acquire a large dog bred to run, you must make sure that he gets chances to run freely. Otherwise he will never expend his pent-up energy and this can result in problems arising elsewhere. Look for a large field with good fencing where you can allow your dog run freely when nobody else is around.

Some hunting dogs come from so-called performance breeding. Performance breeding means that the puppies come from a long line of dogs used successfully for hunting purposes. The owner breeds dogs who show desirable hunting traits, like prey drive. There is a considerable difference between buying a Dachshund, Beagle, Cocker Spaniel, Setter, or Retriever from

An unleashed Sighthound can cover a lot of ground very quickly.

a hunter versus purchasing one from a breeder whose dogs haven't been used for hunting for generations.

A short note about mixed-breed dogs. I am often asked whether mixed-breed dogs are the healthiest, most devoted, and the least inclined to hunt. While there is some evidence to support the notion of being healthier, you can't assume they are less inclined to engage in predatory behaviors—that is just not the case. Let's assume, for example, you have a Beagle (who can track very well) mixed with a Setter (who likes running and is very fast). You now have a mix of two talented hunting dogs. Not exactly a guarantee of a limited hunting drive. Or let's imagine you have a Greyhound and Labrador mix—why should he be less interested in hunting or more focused on his owners than his purebred parents? If you are interested in a dog that is mixed-breed, simply read the breed description of the parent dogs, assuming this is known, and be prepared for him to have a bit of both in him. No one can really predict how much and from whom—you will discover this when you are living with the dog. Friends of mine have a Terrier and Dachshund mix who has absolutely no interest in hunting and happily trots alongside them during walks in the forest. Oh well, that's a mixed-breed for you.

Body language/expressive behavior of the dog

The body language of a dog is infinitely varied, interesting, and can give clues as to when he is likely to engage in chase and predatory behaviors. The way he holds his head and tail, what he does with his eyes, ears, fur, the posture, the look—all this is worth understanding and working out how it fits together. An erect stance with eyes intently focused on a particular target could be an example of interested observation or eye stalking potential prey, depending on the situation and other physical cues.

The senses at work

Have you ever noticed how your dog uses his senses? Most people are surprised to learn that in order to track prey dogs first use their eyes, then their ears, and only finally their strongest sensor, the nose. A dog first tries locating prey on a visual or auditory basis. Only when this is unsuccessful does he try to find a scent trail he can follow. The reason for this is that dogs always try to get to their prey using the method that requires the least amount of work because, in the wild, it is necessary to utilize their energy in the most efficient way possible. The least strenuous thing to do is to first see if a potential prey animal can be spotted. Using the ears to listen closely for rustling or cracking in the undergrowth also does not require any major effort and only a tiny amount of energy. The dog is most physically challenged when he must concentrate on following a track, particularly when it is a few hours or days old and leads through difficult terrain.

A dog uses his eyes and ears to locate prey before resorting to his sense of smell.

Observe your dog carefully. Can you develop a feel for when he is on the lookout for prey? As soon as he gives an indication, you should either put him on the leash or give him an alternative task to do. In the following chapter, you will read about teaching your dog alternatives to chase and prey behaviors, learning more appropriate tasks, and which commands are the most practical to use. Let's focus on some important elements of expressive behavior as shown in the next set of photographs. Knowing what the dog's body language is indicating should help you anticipate and interpret chase and predatory behavior more accurately and, where possible, intervene more effectively.

This dog's tail is held vertically, one front leg slightly bent, the snout pointed and sniffing the air, and a look of concentration—a prey animal cannot be very far away.

This Giant Schnauzer is excitedly following a scent with his nose close to the ground. The erect tail clearly shows his tense concentration.

A young Vizsla, concentrates on the ground in front of him. Soon, he'll spring into the "mouse pounce" or start to dig enthusiastically, most likely for a small prey animal.

If a dogs points with a bent front leg, he suspects that a prey animal is to be found in that given direction or he has already seen it.

This dog is sniffing with a tense posture. When this photo was taken, both the owner and I were glad he was on-leash because, as you can see by the tight leash, he would have given anything to see what was hiding in the bush.

Predatory motivation is connected to hunger

Predatory motivation is to a large extent (but not exclusively) controlled by hunger. You should make sure that your dog is fed on a consistent and adequate basis. That does not mean you should feed him until he's fat and rotund, nor should he automatically get something every time he indicates he is hungry. And certainly it does not mean that an over-fed, fat dog will not chase game animals or anything else he perceives as prey.

The following is an example of how appetite can contribute to prey behavior. A few years ago, a farmer's wife called me for advice because her German Shepherd was crazy about hunting. Repeatedly, the dog had practically emptied a neighbor's chicken coop and this caused a lot of trouble with the neighbor as well as with her husband—who had been against getting a dog in the first place. I asked how often the dog went on chicken raids and she told me that it had occurred eight times in the last few weeks. At the beginning she had only killed one or two chickens, but now was killing any she could catch that were running around.

As soon as the neighbor placed more chickens in her yard, the dog would begin to stalk. She managed to get over a pretty high

A yard full of chickens is very tempting to a hungry dog.

fence and even a subsequent beating would not stop her from trying to get to chickens—and successfully, at that! There was no point in locking her up because she found her way out again and again. If there were no chickens to be had, she provided for her own meals by running into the forest, often coming back to the farmyard with wild prey in her mouth.

My interest was piqued and I decided to make a house call to assess the situation myself. It seemed to be very unusual that the dog returned home with prey in her mouth. Although she knew full well that she would be in trouble with her owners when she got back, she continued to bring prey home.

When I arrived at the farmyard, I was led to the kennel in which the dog was kept. What I saw quickly and unmistakably clarified the situation. I saw an emaciated dog who had six puppies! The food bowls were all empty and when I inquired, after a few excuses, the farmers admitted that they had seldom fed the dogs. That's why she *had* to go hunting and get food—she had to secure the survival of herself and her puppies!

I explained to the owners that their behavior had practically forced the dog to go searching for prey—whether next door in the chicken coop or in the forest—and that we would most definitely not be able to change this behavior as long as the dog wasn't fed adequately. I questioned them further and they confirmed that the dog had not chased game animals before she'd had puppies. This gave additional support to my theory, since previously she had run around the farmyard without showing the slightest interest in the neighbor's chickens. After this, a heated exchange of words broke out between the couple about the sense of keeping a dog, that the "stupid mutt" only caused trouble and expense, and that there was no guarantee they would find buyers for the puppies.

From all of this, one thing was clear to me—both the dog and her puppies needed help. I painted a picture for the people in the most vibrant colors what trouble they would get into if the dog emptied the chicken coop again—which she would most certainly do—and that it wasn't worth a neighborhood war breaking out.

The story ended with me temporarily adopting the dog and her puppies. I put them in a friend's garden shed, fed them properly, took care of and trained them, and let them play in a fenced area. When the puppies were old enough, we found them homes. The German Shepherd got a new name and a home with a friend of mine. Thanks to training and foresighted and careful ownership, her hunting drive has been brought under control and there have been no further incidents.

CHAPTER 2
TRAINING FUNDAMENTALS AND EQUIPMENT

In this chapter, I will present the fundamentals underlying the training techniques and equipment I have used for many years and which I have had the most success dealing with chase and prey behaviors. When putting training into practice there are a number of things to consider:

- A training program consists of many individual elements that can only lead to the desired success when used as a whole. In other words, if you do only nose work and communicative walks, for example, you will not be successful in keeping your dog from engaging in unwanted predatory behavior, especially if your dog's prey drive is extremely pronounced. If you work on all, or at least most, of the elements of the training program, you will have a better chance of success.

- Don't expect miracles from yourself or your dog! This training requires sensitivity, patience, consistency, foresight, and ultimately experience. You can't achieve this overnight. Don't approach it with too much ambition. Give yourself and your dog plenty of time and have fun together!

- Be prepared for setbacks. They will often occur after an initial success, especially if you get a little careless in your training.

- Keep a training diary. If you write down exactly what was trained and when and how your dog reacted to it, you will find the sources of failure quickly if the training is not successful. My training diary has proven itself to be a valuable aid for finding sources of failure. I also like to use it if dog owner clients are desperate and believe their dog is not making any progress at all. When they go back through the diary, it quickly becomes clear that their dog's behavior has, in fact, improved.

Elements of training

Your own body language

If you are out walking with your dog and you see anything he might take to be prey, it is important for you to stay calm and not become tense. If whenever you spot a deer or jogger, you startle or immediately pull the leash back, you will give your dog a signal that prey might be near by.

The same occurs if you constantly expect things to appear that your dog might chase. If you always walk slowly and are constantly looking around, it looks as if *you are searching for prey animals in your dog's eyes.* I have observed dog owners during training who walk through a forest or over fields, always uncertain and on the lookout, all the time being watched with great interest by their dogs. The moment the owner comes to a stop, or looks intensely in a particular direction, the dog registers it and immediately checks to see if prey has been spotted somewhere. You will compound this mistake by pursuing a dog once he's already run off. The dog can easily misinterpret that as, "Oh fantastic, my human is running with me, we're hunting together."

A relaxed posture communicates calmness which carries over to the dog.

Proper tone of voice

The proper use of tone of voice is incredibly important. And by tone I mean both sound and mood. Your voice can convey a wide variety of emotions, both consciously and subconsciously. So it is also important when you discover a potential prey animal (or a bicyclist or a running child) that you don't call your dog excitedly or become frantic. Rather, remain completely calm and call him to you as if nothing has happened. If you call your dog with a loud and flustered voice, you communicate that something unusual or exciting is happening. He will immediately look around to see what is going on.

Another advantage of using a calm and quiet voice is that dogs are genetically hardwired to pay attention to low sound volume. Why? Because prey animals are generally quiet. Think about the rustling when a mouse makes its way through the leaves, the breaking of twigs when a larger prey animal runs through the thicket, and so on. If you make a quiet sound with your voice, your dog will turn toward you, concentrating. Try it. You'll be surprised by how well it works.

You can practice this easily while out for a walk. When your dog runs a little bit ahead of you, use a quiet sound such as "Pssst." When your dog turns to you to find out where the sound is coming from, praise him and give him a treat. Then step on a twig so that it breaks. As soon as your dog turns around to see who or what caused that sound, praise him and then give him a treat. Later rustle the leaves at a moment when he's not looking, make another noise such as a whistle. Whenever your dog turns around to see where this sound is coming from, praise him enthusiastically and give him a treat. Soon, you will have a dog who will first look to you every time he hears a sound.

Act instead of reacting

Here is another important training element that you should observe: act instead of react. That seems obvious and simple, but it's not always the case, especially when it comes to predatory behavior. Basically, you should find a way to stop the behavior when it first starts or, even better, not allow the dog to get into situations in which he gets the chance to act it out and, by doing so, to perfect it. Not letting it happen in the first place is called management.

Of course it's not always possible for an owner to be the *first* to spot potential prey and intervene accordingly. If you walk around with a high level of concentration, you may be quick to spot squirrels or bicyclists. However, when it comes to smelling or hearing prey, humans cannot, by any stretch of the imagination, compete with dogs. In other words, even if you are very attentive, you will not always be the first to notice prey. For this reason, you should always walk your dog on-leash when you go for walks in areas where game animals, cats, chickens, bicyclists, or running children can be expected to appear.

This clever cat instinctively remains still while watching a nearby dog. He "knows" the dog is more likely to chase him if he starts moving.

Food rewards

The proper use of food rewards is very important to the success of the training you will be learning to counter chase and prey behavior. Here are two important points to remember:

1. Food rewards are only given for actions that have been correctly performed. This is not about stuffing the dog full

of treats just because he is "so sweet" or you don't know how else to get his attention.

2. When introducing a new behavior, reward every single step until the dog understands the whole sequence. Once he does, reward him only at the end of the action. Ultimately, reward the dog in a *variable* (and for the dog, non-obvious) pattern. Sometimes give him a treat, at other times praise him, or simply let him do something that he enjoys. Behavioral research has shown that variable and intermittent rewards are the most motivating. This is true not only in dogs, but also in humans.

This is a good spot for a brief digression to give you an example that illustrates the power of food rewards. I have several horses that I keep in a rented stall. I occasionally help the owner of the stall with odd jobs and, one day, she placed a piece of chocolate on my desk. I found it and was, of course, delighted. When I returned to the stall the next day, there was another piece of chocolate from her, this time tied to the hay fork I use to distribute the morning feed to the horses. I was surprised and really touched by this lovely idea. When I entered the stall on the third day, I was already looking forward to possibly finding a piece of chocolate somewhere—and I found it, this time tied to the water faucet. This went on for a few days and each day I drove to the stall thinking about where I was going to find the chocolate that day. On the sixth or seventh day, I didn't find any. I was disappointed, but drove to the stall the next day with even more excitement about whether I would, or would not, find something *today*. Deep in these thoughts, I just had to laugh. That's how intermittent rewards work, I thought. When I *always* get something, it becomes a matter of course. If I never get anything, I don't have any incentive to carry on performing *well*. And it's the same with dogs.

I always find it a disappointment when dog owners are so unimaginative in preparing treats and simply stuff a bit of dry food into their pocket just to have *something* on them. If you only had pasta every day and then someone gave you some more pasta for doing something well, how would you feel about that? Wouldn't you prefer to have chocolates? And which of the two would motivate you more?

Choose treats your dog really likes. That does not always mean what you think he likes. Ask him what he really likes. And how should you do that? Simple. Take four or five different things that you believe your dog likes—perhaps sausage, cheese, dry food, a piece of pancake, some pasta, or whatever. Offer your dog one item in your left hand and another in the right hand. Observe which hand he shows more interest in, that is, which one he prefers. Then do this with all the types of food until your dog has indicated the one or two which he really prefers. Use these for your training.

For training, use treats your dog really likes.

If your dog has done something really well, give him a jackpot. That means that he gets lots of his favorite treats one right after the other—that way, the after-taste lasts longer. A few weeks ago, I trained with a young dog in a forested area that was heavily populated with deer, badgers, foxes, and many other animals. She had already learned to sit on command when another animal appeared, but today she demonstrated that she fundamentally understood the task. When we came around a bend and we saw a deer in the field, she sat herself down and looked toward me! Well done—jackpot!

Do not let yourself be deterred by people who are of the opinion that your dog shouldn't get any treats because he should work willingly for his human and not for food. Giving food is a quite natural form of reward because even in the wild, dogs "work" to get nourishment. If used correctly, it is very useful and effective in getting the kinds of behavior you want from your dog.

I have thought long and hard about what possesses people to believe that a dog should want to please them, i.e., be willing to perform behaviors without some sort of more tangible reward. It could just be arrogance, or could it be the deep down desire of a human to have at least one living being in this world that loves him unconditionally? Why do we believe we can demand from our dogs what we are not prepared to give in our human relationships? We don't love unconditionally, either. Would you live with a person who you didn't get anything from, neither emotionally nor financially, nor in terms of respect, nor anything else? We all want something for ourselves, which is socially accepted and, of course, perfectly okay. I would most definitely not want to live with a partner (whether two or four-legged) if I didn't get *anything* out of it.

Probably the most interesting variation on this theme is a comment I frequently hear from most dog owners: "Yes, he is easily bribed," when the dog is offered and takes a treat from me. The accusation of corruptibility is not exactly a compliment. I then ask a question, "When you work the whole month and get your salary at the end of the month, are you taking a bribe? Or, to put it another way, if you worked for a month and your boss offered you money for it and you declined to take it, would you demonstrate a better character than your colleague who took his salary?" The answer is mostly, "Well, if you put it that way…" Yes, that is how I put it. It is perfectly okay for a dog to get an appropriate reward for good behavior.

Introducing distractions

When you begin training, do it in an area that offers few or no distractions. A distraction is anything that might draw your dog's attention away from what you are trying to get the dog to do. Distractions include things such as other dogs or people, or even just a different location filled with different sights, sounds, and smells. Only after your dog has completely learned an exercise in a safe environment do you begin to *gradually* increase the level of distractions. Don't expect too much at once. Don't expect the high school diploma after the first class in elementary school. You have to learn to be a good teacher—and that means that you gradually raise the level of difficulty of the tasks so that your dog makes the least number of mistakes possible and can go from one small success to the other.

Even training two dogs together is a form of distraction. When dogs can learn behaviors with distractions, they have earned a nice treat.

Do not—under any circumstances—let yourself be talked into the targeted use of distractions to entice the dog into showing an unwanted behavior, only so that you can punish him. Basically, this is setting him up to fail. It doesn't make any sense and above all it is unfair to tempt the dog into disobeying and then punish him for not completing a task. Imagine teaching school children in such a way—constantly giving tasks with the intention of making them fail in order to correct them with punishment. You would shake your head in disbelief at the stupidity of such a teacher.

Recommended training equipment

Generally, I am not the biggest fan of lots of training equipment. A lot of the kinds of training devices that purport to help with unwanted chase and prey behaviors are frequently ineffective at best, utterly nonsensical, or involve animal cruelty at worst. You will find out more about the products to avoid in Chapter 6. For me, the two most important training aids are a good everyday leash and a field leash combined with a harness.

A good leash

The one piece of training equipment you absolutely need is a good leash. Such a leash allows you to keep your dog under control and is an invaluable training aid when used correctly.

A good ten foot leather leash.

I recommend a ten-foot length leash made of leather or high-quality nylon. Don't scrimp on the price when buying a leash because it doesn't pay off in the long run. Make sure that the material is soft so that you do not injure yourself if you have to quickly grab hold of the leash in an emergency or the leash slips through your fingers. It shouldn't be shorter than ten feet because you want your dog to be able to move around you in a reasonably sized radius without the leash immediately going taut. Furthermore, you want him to have the chance to sniff on either side of you without pulling. In urban areas that are more congested, you can simply shorten the leash or switch to a seven-foot leash.

Recognize that the leash does not replace communication! Frequently, dog owners make the mistake of paying less attention to the dog and not giving him any clear instructions when he is on-leash because they think he can't run away. So instead of a nice relaxed walk together with plenty of communications, often a picture emerges of a dog who is practically dragged along on his leash by his inattentive owner. Recently, while out walking, I observed a young woman who was pulling her West Highland White Terrier behind her while he was trying in vain (but urgently) to sit down so that he could relieve himself. It wasn't that she didn't care, and I'm sure she didn't mean to just keep pulling him along, but she wasn't paying any attention as she was obviously lost in thought. I talked to her and she thanked me politely for the tip and stood still so that her dog could relieve himself.

It is important for you to give your dog enough freedom of movement through using an adequately long leash. This way he can have a really good sniff and go off road from time to time to discover new things.

What you should strive for is to establish communication with your dog so you don't always need to use a leash to keep your dog close to you. Show him with the appropriate verbal or hand signal the direction in which you would like to go. Talk to him if you want to stop after walking for a while and then let him know when it's time to move on.

If your dog is frequently on-leash when you go for a walk, sometimes make the extra effort to find a safe place where you can let him off the leash. Let him walk a bit in a field and wait for him if he really wants to have a thorough sniff. If he is always expected to walk on-leash next to you at the same speed and on the same side of you, he won't get much enjoyment from his walk.

On the other hand, don't let yourself be put off by people who try to convince you that a dog should never be on-leash, because that isn't true either. Your dog will get enjoyment from walks if you can keep him under control while he moves about freely within a generous leash radius.

If you want to let your dog off-leash, *absolutely* make sure that he has completely learned the Sit and Stay behaviors covered in Chapter 4, and you can keep him near you unless you release him to run freely. That's why I always make a point to use release command with a calm voice. I have observed dog owners too often who say with an excited voice "Off You Go!" when they take the dog off the leash, and the dog then really shoots off. Mood transfer travels—as previously mentioned—in all directions. So keep in mind that your training should not encourage your dog to shoot off like a rocket the moment he hears the click of the clasp (even if it is fun to watch!).

A typical field leash.

The field leash

In addition to your everyday leash for walks on paths, I recommend a longer "field leash" for use in fields and forested areas. For these occasions, I use a field leash with a length of 30 feet. Even longer leashes of this type are available, but in my experience, they are very cumbersome as they are apt to get knotted or tangled. Furthermore, I want to have the dog close enough to me so that I can work with him. If he is running 60, 90, or even 120 feet ahead of me, it is much more difficult to keep him under control using verbal or visual signals.

The same general criteria in terms of quality and softness apply to both the ten-foot leash and the field leash. I strongly recommend getting a good leather field leash, no nylon in this case. The initial cost is maybe two or three times higher than a nylon leash, but this investment is paid back ten-fold due to the durability of the material. Furthermore, nylon or cotton web leashes suck up a lot of water when they get wet so they can become very heavy. Twigs, stones, leaves, and so on get caught in the material, and it tends to fray as it is dragged along the ground, adding unnecessary weight and making your hands dirty while you are working.

When first starting out with a field leash, stick to working with your dog in open areas where you can always see him for ease of handling. After you have had experience with such a long leash, you can move to more forested areas where there are more obstacles to negotiate. Hold the strap in your hand and let the leash drag along the ground. After all, you want to increase his freedom of movement and you can achieve this only when you allow him the entire length of the leash.

You must, however, be very attentive when you walk because if your dog actually sees prey and decides to take off running, you may have to shorten the leash very quickly. You can do this either by grabbing hold of the leash closer to the end or very rapidly rolling it up. If your dog runs to the end of a thirty-foot leash, you'll receive a jerk in your spine that you will most definitely—and painfully—notice. If you have a large, strong dog, you could be knocked off your feet.

Never let go of the end of the leash! A field leash is not there to just be attached to the end of the dog while he moves uncontrolled across the ground. That is much too dangerous. Over a period of years, I have taken part in searches for many dogs who ran off with their field leashes dangling wildly behind them—and became stuck in brush wood, on buildings or somewhere else, they were not able to free themselves from. We searched for Jacko, a Munsterländer, for three days before we found him completely distraught on a haystack under which the leash had caught on wooden slats. Moses, a shorthaired mixed-breed from Portugal, was worse off. In winter, with temperatures around 50 degrees, he ran after a deer at 4 p.m. and disappeared into the forest. When his owner still had not found him at 8 p.m. and the thermometer had meanwhile dropped to just above freezing, she called me and asked me to help her search for him. Around 8:45 p.m. I met up with a group of dog owners at the "point of departure" and we started to search for him. At 11:30 p.m. we found Moses, extremely frozen, shivering and shuddering over his entire body. The temperature had meanwhile dropped to just below freezing. His field leash had become entangled in a bush and he couldn't get himself free. We took him immediately to a vet who told us he would not have survived the night—maybe not even one hour longer—out there.

A leash attached to a harness is a good option for all dogs.

If you have a dog who—at least some amount of the time—has to walk on the field leash, you should absolutely make sure that he is fitted with a harness. In general, using a harness instead of a collar is preferable, but if your dog is on a long leash, it is vital. The danger of injury that a dog is exposed to is extremely high when he reaches the end of a leash with fifteen, thirty, or more feet. The entire pressure of the jerk he receives when he hits the end of the line is distributed across the cervical spine, larynx, thyroid, and trachea. You can compare this to the impact of crashing into another car at about 35 mph. Remember: we humans put the seat belt across our chests and don't wrap it around our necks—and for a good reason. In my opinion, wearing a harness is always more sensible than wearing a collar—in field leash training it is indispensable!

Rules for using a field leash:

- Never let go of the end of the leash.
- Concentrate when you go for walks, so that you can shorten the leash if necessary.
- Combine the field leash with a well-fitting harness.

Ready for a nice walk with a field leash and harness.

CHAPTER 3
COMMUNICATIVE WALKS AS A KEY TO TRAINING SUCCESS

Except when a dog gets (or is let) loose from his home, going out on walks will likely be his best chance to engage in chase and predatory behaviors. While on a walk, the owner might let the dog off-leash or the dog might pull free while on-leash and, before he can be stopped, he is off on a chase. So you might ask, "Why should we go for walks together if the key to successful training is to help curb this behavior?" The key is learning to go for what I call communicative walks.

When you go for a walk with your dog, you should make sure that you really go for a walk *together*. By together, I mean using the walk as an opportunity to build a strong bond between you and your dog though interaction and communication. If you do so, your dog will focus more on you than on the surrounding environment and will be more likely to respond to you than what he perceives to be potential prey. *When your dog chooses to focus on you because he finds it rewarding to do so, you have a dog who is less likely to choose to engage in chase and prey behaviors.* The techniques used on communicative walks will help convince your dog to focus on you, but only if you focus on him.

Focusing on your dog

It is often the case that an owner is lost in his own thoughts or deep in conversation with someone else while his dog does his own thing during a walk. He sniffs, marks, runs a bit, digs, climbs on and off something, finds a very valuable treasure like a bone, plays with other dogs, and/or runs ahead. Meanwhile his owner only talks to him when he is either giving him a command or forbidding him from doing something. The dog learns quickly to stay away from his owner and to go his own way. Even attempts at visual or physical contact by the dog often go unanswered, or go unnoticed by the owner. If the dog eventually stops these attempts, people say he would not have a good bond to his owner.

Have a good look at two or more dogs who go for walks together. You will become aware that the dogs often make contact with each other, although in a much different manner from how we humans do it with each other. When two people go for a walk, they generally talk a lot with each other. The communication between them is to a large extent determined by speech, with the spoken word being augmented by gestures and facial expressions.

Take the time to communicate with your dog frequently while out on walks.

With dogs, it is quite different. Their communication is to a large extent determined by eye contact and tactile communication—through touching. Of course, communication also occurs through barking, whimpering, whining, howling, and many other sounds that dogs use to tell each other what's going on. But vocal utterances overall comprise a considerably smaller portion of their communication than what we humans use with each other.

Additionally, it is worth considering that dogs generally do not understand our words. Of course, they can learn that the same expressions delivered in the same tone and used in the same context always mean the same things. Most dog learn, within a short space of time the meaning of expressions such as "Do you want to go for a walk?" or "Do you want your goodnight treat?" or "I'll be right back." But phrases like "I've told you a 100 times that you shouldn't go running after rabbits and no you're not a good dog, you're a bad dog and I don't like you anymore." This, of course, they do not understand.

We can't really teach a dog our language, but with a bit of thoughtfulness and care, we can learn parts of theirs! And we can learn to communicate with them through joint activities. It is not just fun. It creates an extremely strong bond. This bond is one of the basic requirements for being able to recall a dog shaking with excitement when he spots a deer in a meadow or a rabbit tearing off across a field.

Activities to engage in while walking

Finding activities to engage in while walking with your dog adds fun to your communicative walks, can act as training opportunities, and, most importantly, continue to build the bond between you and your dog that will help minimize his desire to chase prey. Here are some of the things I frequently use in training and have been greeted with enthusiasm by most dogs.

Eye contact

This simple exercise can be done on any type of walk. Train yourself to notice how often your dog makes eye contact with you. You will find that he does it more often than you may have previously thought. If he runs ahead a bit, for example, it's almost a guarantee he will turn his head occasionally and look back at you. Return his gaze. Give him a nod, a treat, or make a hand gesture in the direction you would like him to go. You can also say something like "Well done," but you don't need to create a big fuss every time he looks at you—it is enough when he notices that you are also watching out for him as much as he is for you! And you should most definitely not ask for a behavior every time your dog makes eye contact.

Most dog owners are very surprised when they notice how often their dog makes eye contact with them when they start to watch for it. At the same time, they realize how much they had previously neglected it and had lost an opportunity to reinforce it.

Tactile contact

As mentioned above, tactile contact comprises a considerable part of canine communication. Have you ever noticed that, during a gentle walk on a relatively wide path, your dog will pass very close to you and often brushes against your leg as he goes by? This is no accident. The dog knows exactly how wide the path is and where you are standing. It is his way of saying: "Hello, nice of you to be here, I'm just going a little bit further ahead…"

A few years ago I trained with a Do Khyi dog named Wutjen. During the training walks that we went on with Wutjen, she would come running up to us from behind again and again, softly nudging her nose into the back of her owner's knee. Then she would look up with a "smile" on her face and run on. I observed this for quite a while and finally Wutjen also did it with me. I was really delighted about this and had the feeling I had now been admitted into the inner circle of *her* people. As she looked at me, smiling, I smiled back and started a short mutual run and catch game. Wutjen was delighted.

Her owners asked me what this nudging meant because they had also noticed she often did it during walks, but only with people she knew and liked. I explained to them that this was Wutjen's way of making friendly contact and demanding that they do something together. They reacted to me with disbelief and so I proposed a test. If my hunch about Wutjen's behavior was right, she wouldn't nudge us as much once we interacted more with her during walks. And that was what happened. Wutjen is now an old lady, but she still nudges her humans in the knee with her large Do Khyi nose from time to time. It is her way of saying: "Hello, let's do something together."

You too can use tactile communication when you're out with your dog. For example, if he has stopped to sniff along the edge of a path, stroke him with the back of your hand while you go by. Don't say anything, just carry on walking. When he looks at you, just look at him and enjoy this moment of togetherness. It is also completely okay if he then carries on sniffing because it is not the aim of this exercise for him to stop doing so. It's simply about getting his attention for a short moment, even when he is in the middle of sniffing something.

A dog will often nudge your leg while walking. This should be acknowledged.

Of course, you can also just stand still and pleasantly ask your dog to come to you and then stroke him or cuddle him. When the weather is fine, during a walk I often sit down in the grass (or in winter on dry snow), collect my dogs around me, and look at the landscape. At such times, two of my female dogs love to sit pressed up against my back while Chenook, my large male dog, wants to have his ears massaged and grunts with pleasure when I do so.

Finding a sausage tree

This exercise will be the one your dog will have the most fun with and is very beneficial in terms of you being able to keep your dog under your control.

Take the time to stop and cuddle or stroke your dog while out for a walk.

Go out alone before you walk your dog. Take the route you plan to go on with him and deposit lots of pieces of sausage on a bush, in the bark of a tree, or in the crevices of a rock. Prepare the tree in such a way that a few sausage pieces are placed high enough that your dog won't be able to reach them without your help. Then fetch your dog and head out on your walk. When you get close to the "sausage tree" call out excitedly, "Look what I've found!" and show your dog your sensational discovery. Generally, dogs finding such a prize in this manner for the first time are amazed. They sniff carefully, look inquisitively at their human, and then delicately try to pluck the sausage pieces. Praise your dog when he does that. When he tries unsuccessfully to get to pieces you have placed up high, help him by carefully bending the branch down to him so that he can reach them.

There are three important benefits to this exercise. First, the dog begins to think that "when my human calls me all excitedly, he's definitely found a sausage tree. I'm coming!" For this reason, the exercise is ideal for dogs who have learned to associate your excited voice with prey, a common problem if you tend to get excited if you see prey and try to keep your dog under control. One of my clients was always frustrated that, when she spotted a hare and recalled him in a flustered voice, her dog knew straight away that a hare had to be somewhere nearby and so ignored her calls. We established the exercise with the sausage tree and her dog learned that when his owner called really excitedly, it was more likely to be a sausage tree than a hare!

Secondly, sausage trees are only to be found with the owner present at the scene. The dog learns to associate this wonderful find with his owner. In other words, he learns it is more worthwhile to remain by his owner than going out alone to search in the forest.

Third, some pieces of sausage are always hung in such a way that the human has to help the dog get them. The dog needs help and learns that he needs his human around to obtain all the sausage. That deepens the bond between you and your dog.

Place a sausage in the bark of a tree, then help your dog find it.

43

This exercise, while quite simple on the surface, is one of the core elements of my training efforts. I have gotten dogs who were staring intensely into the distance, watching a few deer, to come back to me by calling excitedly, "Look what I've found." A sausage piece in the mouth is better than game animals far away—if not for all, then for most dogs.

Finding a "sausage tree" when out for a walk with you is a bonding experience.

When and where to go for communicative walks

A communicative walk is something more than just a casual quick trip around the block or a brief foray outside with your dog to retrieve the morning newspaper. As you will see in the remainder of this chapter, I am going to recommend that you engage in a number of activities with your dog to help build a stronger bond and improve your communicative skills with your dog. These will give your dog a greater incentive to stay with you. Recognize also that I live in a relatively rural area and the walks I take with my dog reflect that. If you live in a more urban area, you may need to seek out parks or other open areas to get the full benefit of these exercises, at least initially. For the most part, I recommend that the dog be off-leash on these communicative walks.

Consider when and where you go for walks. Think about the time, for example. Most prey animals are active at dusk or when it is dark. Tracks are freshest in the morning. For a dog with a strong prey drive, you shouldn't begin walking at dawn in a forest that is teeming with prey animals.

If at all possible, go for walks in areas that are not familiar to your dog. In general, a dog is more interested in staying in contact with his owner in unknown terrain than he is during his morning run where he could easily find his own way home. In addition, there is the advantage that the dog doesn't know if game animals or other "prey" are present, and if so, where they are. I often observe dogs who, on the home stretch, turn the corner excitedly because they know that they will soon see the barn with the rabbit burrow under it. If you come to a place where you know your dog will see some form of prey, put him on-leash so he does not get the opportunity to engage in a chase.

Learn to watch the environment carefully

If you have a dog who has a strong prey drive, one of the most effective things you can do is to observe your environment carefully because you want to be able to put him on-leash or get him under your control before he discovers potential prey, be it a cat, deer, or a jogger.

Watch for paths used by animals in a forest and put your dog on leash at places like this to avoid temptations.

Forcing yourself to observe and anticipate while walking can actually be quite enjoyable because you become much more aware of your environment. My clients are always fascinated when I explain to them what a worn path, a snapped twig, a smell, or a particular type of scenery can tell us about the game animals present in that area. I learned this during various excursions with hunters who kindly took me on their various forays and taught me about tracking. A worthwhile tip: look out for hunters' stands. They are built where game animals are to be found.

Concentration exercises for the dog owner

One thing is clear—your dog must learn, but you should too. The success of anti-predation training doesn't just depend on how well you train your dog to steer his natural tendencies in an alternative direction—toward you— but also how well you concentrate on the dog as your partner. You should always know where he is and more or less what he is doing. That way you are generally immune to sudden movements or reactions. How well do you focus on your dog? When you go for a walk with your dog, are you focused enough that you can at any point say where your dog is and what he is doing?

Here is an exercise to try. Go for a walk with your dog and a friend who is asked to say, "stop" periodically without warning. As soon as you hear this word, stand still, close your eyes, and point with your hand in the direction in which you think your dog is. Say what you think he is doing—sniffing, digging, urinating, or whatever.

This exercise is more of a challenge if you are walking with more than one dog. Ultimately, it is only a question of practice and a bit like driving an automobile. When you sit in your car with a friend and drive 300 miles, you can concentrate on the traffic and still be able to have a conversation with your passenger. You learn to concentrate on both. And it is exactly the same when going for a walk with your dog. Even when you are having a conversation or you are lost in thought, a part of your attention should always remain on your dog.

Concentration exercises for dog owners don't just provide a welcome change they also make it clear that the dog is not the only one who needs to learn during training.

CHAPTER 4
BEHAVIORS TO MASTER

Your dog does not need to master as many behaviors as you might think for you to be able to control his prey drive. In fact, some are completely unnecessary. Clearly, however, there are some that your dog must learn so you can take him for walks and/or let him move about freely off-leash from time to time. The dog has to master both a Sit and a Stay behavior. He also must learn a number of recall commands and signals that allow you to bring the dog under your control.

As mentioned in the chapter on Training Fundamentals, make sure you begin training in relatively stimuli-free areas and increase the distractions gradually. You and your dog will be more successful if you don't ask for too much too soon.

Pay attention that you only teach behaviors that are truly possible to carry out and are practical in the given situation. For example, if your dog has short fur or no undercoat at all, you shouldn't do any Sit and Down training with him in wet and/or cold weather. He might not carry out the behavior because the weather makes it unpleasant for him to do so. For this reason, for example, I teach two forms of the Come behavior—one *with* and one *without* Sit. When it is raining, cold, or the dog has a disease of the musculoskeletal system, I almost exclusively use the Come behavior without

Begin teaching behaviors where your dog will encounter few distractions.

asking for a Sit as well. That way if a deer or squirrel appears and I want to get him on the leash as quickly as possible, I don't have to negotiate with him about whether he would like to sit down in this weather or not.

I am by no means of the opinion that good obedience is only established when the dog does what I ask of him unconditionally. Good obedience for me involves not only the dog's reliability, but also the attentiveness and the foresighted thinking of the dog owner. An owner should not demand unnecessary or pointless actions of the dog, especially when it is unpleasant for the dog.

Rest vs. movement behaviors

It is not just the dog who has to master performing and implementing but also his human—you! It is important that you know the difference between rest and movement behaviors and know when to use them. The following table will give you an overview:

Rest behaviors	Movement behaviors
Sit, Down, Stay.	This way, Turn around, Forward.
While performing these, the dog rests in a particular position.	While performing these, the dog keeps moving.
The dog must be released by the person handling him, so that the dog knows *how long* he should perform this action.	No release from the behavior is needed. The dog knows that he doesn't need to keep running without stopping when you have told him "This way."
They demand more concentration from the dog because Sit and Down are more difficult to perform than simply going on when distractions are present.	They demand less concentration from the dog during performance. Simply saying "This way" when the distraction is high is easier than sitting. For this reason, movement commands work well when high distraction stimuli are present.

These two dogs were instructed to accompany their owner with the "This way" movement command.

Keep your training positive

Last, but not least, training must *always* be positive! Never call your dog using his learned behaviors if you are angry. Of course there are situations in which you can sometimes use a stricter voice and scold. But never do this when the dog is supposed to follow a command or has already performed the correct action, even if he did something before that you disapproved of. Also, never use a behavior as punishment, or something that leads to punishment! This would teach your dog that obeying a command is sometimes good and sometimes means that trouble is coming. You do not want to have this type of association when your aim is a behavior that is performed both reliably and willingly.

For example, let's assume your dog is running around in a field and you call him. He quickly glances over to you—in other words, he hears you, but then decides to carry on following his own pursuits. When you then say "Come" in an annoyed and stricter voice, you bring your dog into conflict. Your words tell him that he should come. Your voice and body language tell him he had better not.

How can you avoid this conflict? Call your dog in a pleasant and inviting voice. The moment he comes, praise him. If he doesn't come, be a bit more energetic with your voice saying something like, "Come on now, quickly." As soon as your dog shows even the beginnings of the desired command, *immediately* take the pressure out of your voice and repeat it in a praising way, "Fine, very good, look at this, good dog!" In this way, you signal to him that he has now done a good thing and so can expect a pleasant landing.

Stay and sit behaviors

Teaching your dog to stay put—either by holding still in standing position or sitting is obviously a very key skill in countering the urge to chase prey (from small animals to kids to cars). As with the other behaviors, you need to make it rewarding enough for the dog to make the right choice.

Stay

One of the most important exercises is for the dog to learn to Stay reliably on one spot that has been allocated to him. It's not important if the dog sits or stands, so I allow the dog to decide which position he wants to take after I have given him the command. If it is very hot, for example, the dog can choose to lie down. If it is unpleasantly wet and cold, the dog will more reliably carry out the command if he can stand instead of having to sit or lie down and freeze.

When working to achieve this behavior, you should remember the following—give your dog the "Stay" command in a friendly and inviting voice and walk a few steps away from him while maintaining eye contact. Go back to him and reward him when he stays. Repeat these steps a second time and always release the dog from the command with his reward. Remember not

Stay is taught in four steps: (1) give the "Stay" command; (2) back up a few steps; (3) return to the dog; and (4) give him a reward.

53

to scold him if he changes his position—only correct him if he leaves the allocated spot.

As your dog gradually begins to comprehend that he is to stay and wait for you, slowly increase the number of steps over a few days until you can walk away fifteen steps. This may take several days of training. Now raise the level of difficulty again by turning around as you go away from him—again proceed slowly and carefully.

Tips:

Here are some small, but very effective, tips that you can use to help your dog succeed during training:

- When you walk away from him, don't talk to him—that could encourage him to run after you.

- Don't constantly repeat the command while you walk away from him—your dog could easily misunderstand that you expect something else from him when you continually repeat an instruction that he has already performed.

- When you walk back to him, do so slowly and calmly while staying one step away from him—because if you get too near too quickly and only stop when you are really close to him, he may become afraid you are going to step on him, which could make him get up.

- When in the process of teaching this behavior, never recall your dog out of the "Stay" position. Instead, always go back to him and release him from it. That way, he learns to reliably wait to be fetched by you, even when distracted, because he hasn't done it any other way.

- Incorporate distractions slowly and in small doses so that your dog is not overwhelmed by them, but moves from one small success to the next.

By increasing distractions slowly, you should be able to get your dog to Stay in most circumstances. This Stay deserves a yummy treat.

Of course, it may happen that your dog leaves the allocated spot and runs after you and needs to be shown that he did not perform correctly. I recommend you try the following:

- Calmly bring your dog right back to the starting point. He should learn that he cannot secretly move forward.

- Repeat the exercise again at a shorter distance from where he just got up. That is, if you were at eight steps when he ran after you, try it with seven steps. Your dog should be guided as quickly as possible to training success and if the distance was previously too much, try it with a shorter distance. Once he is successful again, go ahead and reward and/or praise him.

- Do not scold him! A dog who is scolded becomes insecure and nervous and, as a result, it is even more difficult for him to carry out the exercise correctly.

You need to be a good teacher for this exercise, too. That means you set the requirements in such a way that your dog can manage them and goes into training full of confidence.

Sit at a distance

The idea here is that, upon a specific verbal command or visual sign, the dog learns to sit immediately where he is without returning to you. If this behavior is properly established, it can be used to get the dog to sit right where he is even if he is some short distance away from you and stay until he is released from the sit.

The prerequisite for training this behavior is the dog has already learned both a verbal command and visual signal for "Sit." There are a number of possibilities for teaching this behavior; however, the simplest and most effective is to have a friend assist you.

Have the dog walk a little bit ahead of you with someone he knows and likes. The leash shouldn't be too long, just enough to allow the dog to be up to three feet away from the handler. Have your friend and the dog move about 20 feet ahead of you, then use the verbal command and visual sign for "Sit" as shown in the photographs below. Then wait a moment. Your dog will most likely turn around, as soon as he hears your voice give the familiar command, and try come back to you assuming he has previously been taught that sitting is done right next to you. The leash will prevent him from doing so. Repeat the command a few times in a friendly and calm manner until he sits voluntarily. The moment he does that, lower the arm you use to give the sign, praise him in a friendly and calm way (not too enthusiastically or the dog will perhaps stand up excitedly) and go to him. Release him from the sit when you are standing in front of him. Repeat this process four to six times until you notice that your dog is gradually starting to understand that he is expected to sit wherever he is and not try to run to you.

Make sure your assistant does not, under any circumstance, speak to the dog. Otherwise, he will learn to wait for this person's instructions. Your dog should concentrate on what you want from him. The assistant should behave passively and just act as a "leash holder" who prevents your dog from running to you.

Also, never recall your dog out of this command. He should learn that he is expected to stay sitting until you are standing immediately in front of him to release him from the command.

Increase the difficulty of this behavior by repeating the training at various distances until you are sure that your dog has learned what it's all about and reliably sits until you move close to him. For example, have your helper extend the leash out to perhaps ten feet while you remain 20 feet away. Then take the dog off-leash and let him move around freely. When he is 30 feet away, give him the command to sit. If he sits, praise him as always in a normal voice, calmly go to him, release him from the sit, and only then give him his reward and praise him enthusiastically. In this way, your dog learns to maintain concentration after sitting and that the exercise is only over when you stand in front of him and release him. Continue to increase the level of distractions while doing this exercise. For example, work on this outside of a fenced park where your dog could face distractions.

This dog already knows a vertically raised arm is a visual sign for "Down at a distance." For this reason, we used a frontal horizontally stretched arm as a visual sign for the "Sit at a distance" command. It doesn't matter what words you use. What is important is that it is easily seen and understood by the dog.

Recall training behaviors

Recall ability is probably the most important behavior for you to teach your dog, especially if he has a strong prey drive. I advise my clients to train a number of different types of recall behaviors with their dogs. Greater flexibility doesn't just bring variety into the training, but with different forms of recall you can also react in a more targeted way to individual situations. Of course, it is important that a particular command always signals the same requested action to the dog.

Recall exercise #1: "To me" = Come with sit

The goal of this exercise is to have the dog *come* to his handler and *sit* after an appropriate verbal command ("To me") and/ or visual signal is given. It is completely unimportant whether he sits in front of his handler or slightly to the side. What is important is the reliability of performance, especially for a dog with chasing issues. Do not insist that the dog sit in such a way that he is practically glued to you. He will soon find this unpleasant as he strains his neck to make eye contact with you. Give him some space so that he can sit comfortably and make eye contact with you easily. Note that this command is one of the "rest" commands and you also need to have a release command. "All done" is commonly used so that the dog knows when it is okay to get up and move about.

Recall exercise #2: "Look here" = Come without sit

The goal here is for the dog to *run* and make brief contact with his handler after an appropriate verbal command ("Look here") and/or visual signal is given. He's not required to sit. This behavior is particularly helpful in bad weather (so sitting would be really unpleasant for the dog) or in dangerous situations where you want to get your dog on his leash as quickly as possible.

If your dog comes to you hesitantly and/or stays at a bit of a distance from you, reassess your body language and voice. Maybe you were too harsh and so your dog is trying to stay out of your way. Try it again with a friendlier voice and take a few steps backward when he comes toward you. Make sure you position your

Come with Sit behavior illustrated. Note that I am not picky about how/when the dog sits.

signal hand to the side of your body so that you don't have to lean forward when the dog approaches you. This way, it's easier for the dog to happily come and get his treat without you looming over him.

The Come without Sit behavior illustrated. His owner uses a friendly, inviting voice, well-balanced posture and fantastic treats in order to give him the optimum motivation to come. Note the dog is not required to sit.

Recall exercise #3: "Psst" = Come in response to a small noise

The dog learns to run to his handler when he hears a specific quietly uttered sound such as a "Pssst." This signal is perfect for situations when you want to work as quietly as possible, such as when there might be a hunter in the vicinity (this could be dangerous). It is also a really nice attention training command.

Establishing the "little noise" is quite simple. Take really good treats (for best results, sausage or cheese) and, while you make this noise, give your dog some of them. Then wait a moment until

Come in response to small noise behavior illustrated. Your dog is taught to turn back to you when he hears the "Psst" sound.

your dog gets a few feet away from you. Make the noise again and praise him the moment he turns around and runs toward you. Give him the treat as soon as he reaches you. Gradually increase the distance and finally also the level of distraction under which you use the signal.

Recall problems

Many dog owners find that teaching a recall behavior is difficult and frustrating, especially with dogs who have strong prey drives. They become annoyed that their dogs do not come when they call them and so end up never letting them off-leash or always keep them tied up. This failure could be due to several mistakes, the most frequent being:

- After the dog is recalled, he is always put on-leash and can't run free anymore. The dog will likely view coming when called as punishment.

- Only attempting a recall when game animals or other prey objects are close by. If the owner's voice is flustered and nervous, the dog learns quickly that indicates nearby prey and that it is more worthwhile looking for something to hunt than return to his owner.

- *Constantly* recalling the dog. A client of mine recalled her dog five times within two minutes. No wonder he didn't come the sixth time—he could hardly get more than ten feet away from his owner before he was recalled again. The truth is, it speaks volumes for his good obedience that he bothered to come five times.

- Constantly recalling the dog using the "Come" command and then asking the dog to "Sit." In most situations it is not necessary for a dog to come *and* sit when simply coming and remaining standing is sufficient. What is happening is that the dog disobeys the command, not because he doesn't want to come to his owner, but because he doesn't want to sit. By the way, this is particularly true of dogs with hip dysplasia, spondylosis, infection of the anal glands, or other diseases that make sitting unpleasant.

Imagine how you would feel if someone were constantly making the same request to you. Wouldn't it at some point really get on your nerves having to do the same thing over and over again countless times a day?

Alignment exercise

Alignment is one of my favorite exercises. The aim of the exercise is for the dog to orient himself toward you as you stand still. It is relatively easy to set up and establish this action as a useful behavior.

Go for a walk in a safe area with your dog off-leash and stand still when he moves a few feet ahead of you. While you wait, stand completely still. Don't call him. Soon, your dog will notice that you are not walking behind him and will turn around to look back. At this moment, without saying a word, take out a treat and hold it by the side of your body so that it can be clearly seen. If the dog is fairly far from you, you can help him by waving your hand a bit, because dogs see things that are moving more easily than static objects. The moment he runs to you, he gets the treat, again without comment, but with a joyful expression on your face. Stay still for a moment and casually give him treats

Shorty and Jule have learned that it's worthwhile to stay near me.

by slightly stretching out your hand. Why do this? Well, the dog has just learned two things—if he doesn't hear his owner's footsteps behind him, it is worth looking for him because he knows he may get a treat for making contact. And, if his owner stands still somewhere for a moment, for example, to talk to someone, it's worth staying close because there may be something good to be had.

My husband and I are often asked how we manage to get our dogs to stay near us while they are off-leash, even when we stand still. This exercise solves the mystery.

Learning to change directions: "This way"
Learning to change directions is a great behavior for any dog. A very simple and effective command to use for this is "This way." The idea is that the dog learns to move in the direction you choose upon being given an auditory and visual signal.

You accomplish this simply by just doing it. In an area with little or no distractions, say to your dog, "Bello, this way," and, with a corresponding hand signal, walk in the direction you have specified. The moment he follows, praise him. When he has come away from something really interesting, give him a treat as well.

Also, give the command when you change direction or, for example, when you take a fork in a path. If the dog makes eye contact with you the moment you are about to change direction, give him the command only through a visual sign, without saying anything. That increases the dog's attentiveness.

Silent change of direction
Another simple and very effective tool is changing direction while out for a walk without saying anything. The idea behind the exercise is to increase your dogs focus and attention on you. On the path, simply turn around, or take a sharp left or right. When your dog notices this and follows you, praise and/or reward him and tell him how nice it is that he's with you again. While you do so, also change speed. Walk really slowly, then quicker, then slowly again, and then jog a bit.

This dog quickly responds to my request to walk "This way."

It's important that you not trick the dog by suddenly hiding yourself! Such behavior has the potential to create problems. Some dogs respond to you leaving the scene without them being aware of it with fear or a sense of abandonment. At best, your dog will think it's some sort of fantastic new game and will run even further ahead in the hope that you will then hide, he will then find you and will get a reward in the form of a treat or enthusiastic praise. Neither of these are what we are aiming to achieve with this training.

Turn around

Turn around is a good behavior to teach if the dog has run far ahead and you want to have him near you again. The dog learns to change direction upon hearing an appropriate verbal ("Turn around") or visual sign. The dog changes directions and comes back into the dog owner's sphere of influence.

This behavior is very easy to establish and is great fun for dogs. Go for a walk and wait until the dog is around 100 feet ahead of you. Then say "Turn around" in a friendly and encouraging voice, turn, and run in the opposite direction. As soon as the dog follows you, praise him loudly and excitedly until he reaches you. Just keep running so that he really builds up momentum before he gets to you. The moment he gets to you, he gets a treat and really enthusiastic praise. Repeat this exercise with little chance for distraction several times a day for five to seven days.

After practicing, test the command without turning around and moving away. As soon as

At this point, the dog is getting far ahead of his owner.

If your dog gets too far ahead, say "Turn around," walk briskly in the other direction, and then give the dog a nice treat when he catches up to you.

the dog hears the now established signal word, turns around, and runs toward you, praise him enthusiastically and give him a whole load of treats when he gets to you. Now you should not need to turn around anymore when you give him the "Turn around" command because he has connected the desired action with the signal word.

Although the running technique is no longer necessary for the behavior to be successful, I still like to use it from time to time because it has a high participation effect with a corresponding, positive mood transfer. And I get an enthusiastic grin from my dogs when they run after me, catch up to me quickly, and are greeted with a big hello or a treat.

This command is well suited to recalling the dog when faced with great distractions. I frequently use it when the dog has already seen a wild animal and is either just about to take off or has already run off. If any command is going to work, it is this one.

It is also a practical way of keeping the dog near you without having to recall him. As with all commands, what is important here is that you don't use it so often that the dog loses interest in it.

Remaining on a path

This is the behavior I teach to avoid having the dog stray too far away from the edge of the path toward a field or undergrowth. I recommend you begin by saying to the dog "On the path" while pointing at the path in front of you. The praise begins as soon as he starts to move back toward the path and continues until he is completely back on the path again.

The trick to this relatively simple behavior is not to use it too soon. For example, I always give the dog the chance to get a *few* feet away from the path, just in case he is looking for a good place to relieve himself. Very few dogs are willing to do this directly on the edge of a path. Most want to go off into grass, moss, or a bush in order to do so. Here again you also need to observe your dog's body language. A dog who is just about to shoot off to pursue a scent has a very fast way of moving, and his body is more tense than in a dog who is just looking for a spot to relieve himself.

I consciously do not use commands such as "Get out of there" or "No, come back" when the dog leaves the path because this choice of words is too aggressive. After all, I want the dog back on the path where I am walking and such negatively formulated and strict commands are not exactly inviting. I prefer to tell the dog what I want him to do in a firm but friendly manner instead of frustrating him with prohibitions.

Move slowly

The idea behind this behavior is that the dog should slow down and stay near you without having to "Heel."

You teach this behavior by saying the word "Slooow" deliberately, calmly, and drawing it out. Then slow the dog down by moving in front of him and using a corresponding hand signal.

Jule is a curious dog and likes foraging. When she goes too far into the under-growth, I bring her back with the "On the path" command.

Most dogs understand very quickly what you want them to do. As soon as he slows down, confirm this with praise and, after he has walked a few steps at this slower speed, release him from the behavior by giving him a signal word, for example, "All done," and take a step back so that the path is free for him.

I like to use this command when I reach a point in the path where I have no clear view and want to inspect it first before I allow the dog to move freely.

After this dog has properly carried out the "Slooow" command, I allow her to go "free" and show her the stream ahead of us. Playing in water is a wonderful reward for her.

Automatic sitting at the sight of prey

The crème de la crème of all my training exercises involves a behavior in which the dog learns to sit *automatically* at the sight of prey and make eye contact with his human. The exercise is easiest to establish with young dogs, but it is also possible with older ones.

To teach this behavior successfully, it is important for the dog to have firmly mastered the Sit at a Distance behavior and to have

Begin training the automatic sitting at the sight of prey behavior with your dog on-leash and close by you.

performed it many times without problems. Now take him *on-leash* to an area where you have already trained that you are sure will contain something your dog will be tempted to chase, for example a park or forest filled with squirrels or deer. As soon as he sees the "prey," stand calm and still, and shorten the leash (to around 4 feet) without pulling on it. Wait and say nothing. It will not be long before the dog looks inquisitively at you as if to say, "Isn't this where I always get a command?" Look at him in a friendly way and wait. Give him time to think. As soon as he sits, give him a treat and praise him gently. After you release him, praise at great length. Repeat the training cycle many times on different occasions and in different places. As soon as your dog sits and makes eye contact with you, he gets a treat. After being released at the end, he is enthusiastically praised.

Ultimate success! At the sight of potential prey animals, Jule sits automatically and asks me what we are to do now.

Now you need a helper again. The helper goes with the dog (on-leash again) into the park and stands still without saying anything as soon as your dog sees a squirrel. When the dog sits, praise him from behind (about nine to fifteen feet), go to him, release him from the sit and give him lots of treats. Repeat this training step many times. Now you've almost reached your goal.

Now have your helper lead your dog toward a squirrel. If your dog sits at the sight of it, hold back on the praise until your dog turns around to you as if to ask, "Where's the praise?" Then praise him calmly, go to him, release him from the sit and give him a jackpot. Lots and lots of treats and praise for this fantastic dog!

Repeat this training many, many times, varying the distance between yourself and the dog, with and eventually without the use of a friend to help. Now the command behavior is reliably fixed.

Common sources of failure in training

Hopefully your dog will learn all the behaviors covered in this chapter. If you are having problems, these are the most common reasons:

- The dog is constantly on call; he can hardly take a few steps without being given a command. It won't take long before he zones out and ignores anything you have to say.

- The same commands are used too often. After the sixth time within three minutes, even the most positive and interesting training becomes boring.

- Attempts by the dog to make contact with the owner are always answered with a command. The dog learns quickly that it's best not to make contact if he wants to avoid being given instructions.

- The idea that the dog should *constantly* have wonderful things to do. A party every day will eventually become too much for the dog.

- Making exercises too difficult too soon so that the dog is doomed to fail. Give him more practice time and introduce distractions slowly and gradually.

- The dog becomes so fixated on a toy that he becomes a "play junkie." It may well be that by constantly playing with a ball or stick you can keep him busy for a while, but at the end of the day, it won't prevent him from chasing prey. On top of this, there is the danger that problems such as prey aggression or lack of interest in social partners could develop.

- The motivation for training is not high enough. This could be due to uninteresting treats, a monotonous voice, or an uninviting posture. Examine yourself first before you look for the failure in the dog. Was your voice really friendly and inviting? Did you bring sausage and cheese (or what-ever your dog prefers) instead of boring dry food pellets? Did your body language express delight about the work together?

- If you can answer all of the above questions with "yes" and your dog still didn't come when called and didn't get enthused about other tasks, you have to take into account that he might be sick or just having a bad day. Give it a rest for the day. If your dog is still unmotivated and lethargic tomorrow, you should go to the vet to rule out an illness as the cause of his behavior. Really hot weather may cause your dog to be listless and exhausted. Here it would be more sensible to do the exercises and tasks in the cool of the morning or evening in order to see if your dog is more lively and interested in what he is doing.

- Something is preventing your dog from fulfilling the given task. This most often occurs with recall training. Sometimes clients tell me, frustrated, that their dog comes when I am doing the training, but only reluctantly carries out the same exercise with them, or even not at all. Most often this has to do with things that the client is not even aware of. Here is an example: a young man was annoyed that his Gordon Setter always came willingly to me when I called him. If he called the dog, the dog came slowly, demonstrating calming signals, as if expecting to be punished. However, the young man was always friendly to the dog and couldn't figure out why he was behaving this way. I could! He was a chain smoker and as soon as the dog came to him, he stroked him enthusiastically on the head with a lit, smoking, stinking cigarette in his hand, which was very unpleasant for the dog.

- Last but not least, the biggest mistake of all: the owner is convinced his dog will not obey (at least, not him). This feeling undermines one's training efforts. Instead of going into the training together with complete confidence and assurance, from the very beginning, the owner expects it will not work. That is exactly how it will turn out! Has this also happened to you? Have you ever wondered why this happens? One reason for this is that you radiate insecurity and fear, which the dog notices and reacts to accordingly. Another is that you have sent him a mental picture of what he will do, but that picture is of your worst fears. Have you ever wondered whether there is such a thing as telepathy between humans and animals? Try it. Call your dog with the firm expectation that he wants to come in order to do something fantastic with you. Concentrate on the picture of him already running toward you, then wait and see what happens.

CHAPTER 5
PLAY AND OTHER ACTIVITIES

Once you and your dog have done the training and mastered the recommended behaviors covered in Chapters 2 to 4, you are well on your way to having a dog that you can control and keep safe, even if he has a strong drive to engage in unwanted chase and predatory activities. In this chapter, I will review some activities you can do with your dog which will compliment and reinforce the behaviors you have taught and strengthen your bond with your dog.

More and more behaviorists and trainers are recognizing that playing with your dog is a great way to build your relationship with him and that play can create wonderful training opportunities as well. A dog who looks upon you as a source of "fun" is more likely to stick with you than to seek out prey. You do, however, have to be careful that your play activities do not inadvertently enhance a dog's prey drive, especially if he is a breed where that is a strong characteristic. Let's take a quick look at those first.

Play activities you may need to avoid

If your dog exhibits a strong prey drive, I strongly advise against frequently throwing balls, sticks, or other objects for your dog to chase and/or retrieve. These prey games (as the name suggests) mimic the predatory sequence, in which the idea is to chase after the "prey," attack, and then grab it. Essentially, your dog is learning to run after the fleeing "prey," which, once caught, leads to the "shaking to death" aspects of prey behavior. For this reason, I take great care that puppies or young dogs I am training do not play this kind of game. It is no problem if the dog plays with objects, carries them around, tosses them into the air, catches them, and then at the end falls asleep on them. However, predatory games in which the dog becomes excessively fixated on, chases after, or becomes worked up by the object should be strictly limited. My preference is that they not be played at all.

Activities like this also cause adrenaline to be released. This hormone influences a number of physical functions. Breathing and pulse rates gets faster, and the metabolic system releases more and more glucose to provide added energy. In other words, adrenaline supports optimum performance readiness and prepares the dog to attack—which makes sense in a real life situation. Your dog is equipped to mobilize all his energy in a split second in order to concentrate on catching prey and cannot tell his body that today, at this moment, it's only a ball or a stick—a decoy. The moment he starts running to fetch the ball or stick, the adrenaline release begins—which also explains why some dogs get so into the game that they become frantic, bark wildly and whimper, or can hardly calm down. Such dogs may end up developing prey aggression quicker.

It is probably the adrenaline release that makes prey games so attractive to dogs. Likewise, many humans seem to enjoy the rush experienced during extreme sports such as bungee jumping or river rafting. Unfortunately, the release of adrenaline doesn't just have a positive effect on the body. It is, after all, called a *stress* hormone. The more frequently the release of adrenaline occurs, the greater the probability that negative consequences such as nervousness, hyperactivity, or diseases connected to stress will develop.

I would also advise you against using the frequently recommended tip of rolling treats along the ground and having the dog chase/hunt them. Realize when you do this you are training fast reflex reactions toward moving (fleeing) prey. A few years ago I was working with a Fox Terrier who had been chasing treats rolling on a path since he was a puppy. The owner had been advised to do this by the breeder in order to distract him from his prey drive. Unfortunately, this achieved exactly the opposite—the dog not only hunted treats rolling on the ground, but anything else that moved, including leaves dancing in the wind.

You will also want to avoid some of the activities that people use to train their dogs to become successful hunting dogs. For example, using what is sometimes termed a "dog fishing rod." This is a long rod with a string to which a feather or a piece of fur from a prey animal is attached. It is dangled in front of the dog to attract his attention. A game ensues during which the object is raised, dropped, jerked to the side, bounced, etc. The dog tries to catch it and if he succeeds, he is praised and receives a treat.

You can see while this activity may indeed be fun for your dog, you may stimulate an unwanted behavior, especially when your breed or mix is likely to display a strong predatory behavior.

Working with the "dog fishing rod" is only appropriate if the dog (such as this German Wirehaired Pointer) is being trained for hunting.

Appropriate play activities

As in the case of communicative walks, you want your dog's play activities to cause him to look to you as a source of fun and rewards. Again, this helps make you a more attractive alternative to engaging in prey activities. There are other benefits to the right kind of play as well. An important one is to offer the dog tasks and activities that physically tire him out and also challenge him mentally. These might include swimming or splashing about in water, searching for hidden treats or objects, balancing on a fallen tree trunk, solving problems, and digging in a sandbox. My favorite play activities involve searching and digging.

Exercises such as balancing on objects forces the dog to concentrate and encourages him to stay close to you. Choose other exercises that are fun to do together that strengthen the bond with your dog and encourage him to stay close to you.

Hiding treats for your dog

In these photos, you see me hiding a few treats in the forest for my Collie female, Franny. I got Franny when she was 10 years old and, at the time of the photos, she had been with me for only eleven days. For this reason, I didn't quite know how far she would move away from me during walks and how strong her motivation to hunt was. So I decided to make our first joint trip into the forest as interesting as possible so that Franny would be convinced that staying with me would be more rewarding than heading off on her own. Franny was totally enthusiastic about my suggestions for joint activities. Finding sausages in the moss is still one of her favorite pastimes and Franny now sticks close by consistently.

Hiding treats in the crevasses of moss is a great game.

You find something

Another activity I recommend is where *you*—not the dog—find something! This is similar to the Sausage Tree concept discussed in Chapter 3. When out walking, just stand still and concentrate on a point in the countryside. Pretend that you are looking at something very exciting—lay your head to one side and, after a while, breathe in deeply as if it were really exhausting to continue the observation. When your dog finally notices this, he will look in the same direction as you in order to find out what it is that is so great to see. As soon as he looks in the same direction, or maybe at you and then into the distance again (he is trying to find out what you have spotted), start walking in the direction of your find while you continue to look toward it. When you arrive at the particular point, secretly drop a really delicious treat of some sort, which you then show your dog as if you had just found it. Your dog will be delighted by what you find and by your ability to discover treats over such a large distance! You are fantastic at finding good things and it's worthwhile following you.

Rewarding a find

This is another searching exercise that once again involves both the owner and dog. In this case, it is a situation that frequently occurs in which most dog owners react instinctively—but wrongly!

Imagine someone goes for a walk with her dog in the forest and he finds a dead mouse or an old stocking. The dog is delighted! What a fantastic treasure! Proudly, he picks up what he sees as a valuable find and carries it around with him. However, as soon as his owner notices this, out comes an energetic "Leave it!" or "Yuck." What has the dog now learned? There are a number of possibilities. He may have learned that it's better not to bring the prey to his human because he then will be forced to drop it after being harshly spoken to and scolded. If his owner goes after him to take the prey out of his mouth, what he has learned is further reinforced and extended by an extra component: "Better run away or swallow it, then it can't be taken away from me." We don't want either to happen.

One time, I went for a walk with Arco, a young hunting dog, and his owner. The dog found a dead mole and proudly picked it up. The owner was just about to scold him when I quickly stopped her. I praised the young dog gushingly and told him what a fantastic thing he had found. At the same time, I stroked him a lot— and looked into the frowning face of his owner. Then I got him to show me his prey and he did this without any objection. He watched me intensely while I held the mole in my hand, making various comments about this wonderful, dead find.

Arco was very happy when I gave the prey back to him. The owner stared at me in disbelief at what I had done. Because I didn't have any time for long explanations, I just said, "I'll tell you all about it in a moment." I then got the dog to show me his prey again, and again he gave it to me without objection. I admired the stinking, slimy mole and gave it back to him again, full of praise. It continued like this a few times and each time I gave it back to him it was accompanied by mountains of praise about this fantastic prey. Finally, I asked him for the prey again and he gave it to me. I then told the owner to watch carefully what I was about to do. Right in front of the dog, I put the mole in my pocket (thankfully, I had a handkerchief to wrap it in) and gave him a load of treats, again accompanied by various comments of praise.

Then, I explained to the woman that her dog had just learned to bring the prey to me at all times and to present it with confidence instead of simply swallowing it or taking off on a wild chase out of the owner's reach. It seemed to make some sense to the owner, but she wasn't exactly happy about the procedure and asked whether it was really necessary to pocket the prey. "Yes," I said. "At least until you get to the next garbage can or can throw it away without the dog seeing you. But if you just dump it or throw it away somewhere, Arco will just try and fetch it. The idea is that he sees that you will exchange the prey for something fantastic." So far, so good.

This dog wanted to show me his catch which I then took in exchange for a treat.

85

A few weeks later my telephone rang and the same client said excitedly, "I finally understood your training today. Guess what happened. Arco found something in the bush and brought it to me enthusiastically. I took it and saw that it was a meatball. I gave him a big reward and put the thing in my pocket. At home, I looked at the meatball again and discovered that it was spiked with razor blades. I don't want to think what would have happened if he'd swallowed it!"

It doesn't have to be this dramatic in order for you to really see the point of the training. If a dog finds, for example, an old cigarette packet or a plastic bottle, and then starts to play with it, I let him do so. He is proud and enjoys it and no damage is done (as long as he does not swallow it!). I praise the dog and share his enthusiasm for his find. Often, I start a game in which I get the dog to sit and stay, take the object away and place it a few feet from him and then send the dog to go and get it. It is very similar to what goes on at an obedience trial.

The dogs have such fun, so why spoil it when the object is harmless? If I then want to have it, by establishing the above training, it's no problem—because the dog has learned I will give him something good in exchange. I often notice that dog owners on principle forbid the picking up and carrying of objects, which is not at all necessary. It is so nice to experience how a dog brings you "his treasure" with pride and—above all—voluntarily and confidently shows it to you and drops it for you. Admiring the object and starting a game with it creates an unbelievably strong bond because friendship also means enjoying the same things.

Digging activities

If you want to give your dog the chance to dig but he is not allowed to do this in your garden, then build him his own digging paradise in a designated location where he can "let his fur down." Build him a sandbox! You can, of course, buy a readymade one. You don't need much—a wooden square and a lot of sand. In this sand box, you can bury a leather bag with treats. Just bury it a little bit. Then encourage him to search for it. At first, you can help him a little bit by putting a bag in a corner

and letting a little bit stick out. When he's dug it out, praise him and give him some treats from the bag. You can do the same with other objects. Your dog will learn that he is to work through the entire sandbox and bring you all the objects he finds in it. Each time he brings you a find, praise him, give him a treat, and send him back to look for more. You will see how much fun your dog will have with this exercise. Terriers and retrievers should be particularly delighted by this game.

Important: When your dog has found all the hidden objects, indicate this to him by showing him your empty hands and saying, "All gone." Your dog then knows the game/work is over. However, don't use the words "leave it" or "stop" or similar commands used to stop him from doing something that is forbidden. You will confuse your dog by offering him something to do, praising him for doing it, and then assigning a word to this action telling him not to do it a few minutes later. A pleasantly spoken, neutral signal word is much more suited to bringing the game to an end.

Encourage your dog to dig in designated locations.

Nose work

You might ask, "Won't nose work just make my dog's prey drive worse?" The answer to this question is an emphatic "No!" Many people feel that the prey drive of a dog would be more pronounced if they did nose work with him because he would learn to recognize and to follow many different scents. But that is not the case because:

- First, we do not teach dogs how to smell—they know that already. A dog recognizes an endless number of smells and will tend to find the source of an interesting smell regardless of his prey drive. With proper training, you can develop this into an acceptable alternative to help minimize predatory behaviors.

- Second, we do not exercise tracking, substance identification, or search and rescue with prey such as deer, rabbit, or squirrels. Rather, the nose work I recommend involves finding human based or treat based scent articles. For example, you allow him to sniff at a carrot and give him a piece of meat. When you repeat this process a few times, the dog quickly connects the smell of the carrot with the imminent receipt of meat. You can actually get the dog to enthusiastically follow a carrot track right through the forest because he knows that this smell will lead him to something far more attractive than rabbit food.

- Third, it is immensely important to offer the dog the chance to act out this natural instinct and drive. What better way to do this than the targeted steering of a talent given to him by Mother Nature in our chosen direction?

- Fourth, nose work doesn't just offer the dog the chance to exercise his body and his physical capabilities, but it also encourages brainwork. A combination of this is what makes both humans and dogs balanced and happy.

- Fifth, I don't know of any other training that is more capable of "welding" the dog and human team together and at the same time building a trusting bond than nose work. The dog can prove what he is capable of and the human learns to trust his dog and to let him lead during the tracking. This is, by the way, a new and very exciting experience for many dog owners.

Nose work allows your dog to act out his natural instincts while building your relationship with him.

Here are some of the kinds of nose work that can be proper outlets for dogs.

Tracking training
The dog follows a track that has been laid out either by the handler or one created by another person. A variation of this is search and rescue work. In this case, the dog follows a track and when he finds the "missing" person, he then indicates his find in some way to the handler. There are a number of ways of indicating a find such as barking or the so-called "recall-find." Many hunting dogs learn to follow a track and to search for game animals that

have either been shot at or injured by an automobile. For the family dog, tracking is a pleasant past time. In this case, the dog receives food or a toy as a reward at the end for finding what is usually an object such as a glove. Of particular relevance to unwanted predatory behavior, is that the dog learns to only follow a scent when he has learned the signal word to do so—what trainers refer to as "stimulus control," in this case, an alternative to running off in an uncontrolled manner chasing prey.

Tracking is a great alternative behavior to prey chasing.

Area searches

In this type of search, the dog is expected to find objects that are deposited over a strictly defined area. You can, for example, use a square area of 150 x 150 feet or a particular section of a forest or a field. The dog learns to work through this area systematically to bring all the objects it finds to his human, and receives a reward for doing so. He can also look for a missing person in this area and bring his human to this person once he has found him.

An area search involves finding an object within a strictly defined location.

Substance identification

Here the dog learns to distinguish a particular smell from others and to indicate this when he finds it. Some better known examples of this are to find explosives or drugs. You could, however, teach your dog to search for foodstuffs to which you are allergic, or he could learn to identify your scent and, for example, to pick your glove from a bunch of others. One interesting and very valuable service for humans is the scenting of cancer cells. Dogs are specially trained to sniff a patient and to indicate if they can smell cancer cells on them. Scientific studies in the US have found out that dogs can even sniff out an illness in the early stages, well before tumors can be medically diagnosed. There are many possibilities to keep the dog busy and active with nose work and I have not known any dogs who were not enthusiastic about the work once they got started with it.

During substance identification training, the dog is praised and rewarded every time he finds and indicates the desired scent, in this case, by sitting.

Learning and problem solving games

Activities that demand a lot of mental energy on the part of the dog are challenging, fun, and can help tire out an overly active dog. A dog can learn many things—basic obedience, tricks, particular tasks, and so on. During training, however, you should ensure that the dog is *challenged* but not *overly-challenged*. Try to correctly assess your dog and give him learning tasks that he can manage. If you overwhelm him with tasks that are too difficult for him, you will achieve the opposite of what you actually intended—instead of a self-confident and happy dog, you will get an unhappy and frustrated one.

The renowned Swedish psychologist and dog trainer, Anders Hallgren, writes on the benefits of giving your dog lots of physical and mental challenges:

> With all of these activities, the dog is mentally and physically challenged and has to replicate the behavioral repertoire of canids living in the wild. Dogs are, like most mammals, active animals. For this reason, they need physical and mental exercise, preferably spread out in several sequences throughout the day. Just as the body needs water and nutrition, the central nervous system needs mental stimulation. Many dogs rest too much because they are dependent on us taking the initiative for most of their activities. In the wild, for example with wolves or wild dogs, the majority of their energy is used for predation. As we do not want this behavior in our domestic dogs, the energy must be channeled to other activities such as walks, games, and training. That is why it is important for your dog to (occasionally) run at high speed without a leash so that he gets the opportunity to run as far as his heart desires, to romp, to jump, to slow down, to speed up, and so on. A dog must have the opportunity to fulfill his urge to move. (Taken from *Mental Activation—Ways to Stimulate Your Dog's Brain and Avoid Boredom*. Cadmos, 2008)

All predators are natural problem solvers. In the wild, strategies have to constantly be developed for how to find and outmaneuver prey. The trick here is to not only build upon the dog's natural inclinations, but to offer the dog alternative activities to chasing and finding prey to use and nurture his intellect. For example, let him try to open a box containing treats or let him solve the problem of how to get a large stick through a doorframe that is too small for it. In this way, the dog's concentration will be called upon and nurtured.

Games like this provide excellent mental stimulus for dogs.

Obedience and physical exercise

Along with the training for basic obedience and communicative walks, you should absolutely make sure that your dog gets a lot of exercise and is happy. One of my favorite things to do with my dogs is to have them physically balance themselves on all sorts of things. Let your dog work on an obstacle course or jump from one bale of hay to another. He could balance on a tree trunk that is lying on the edge of the path, or jump onto a wall (as long as it's not too high!).

All of these games and exercises give your dog alternatives to engaging in chase and prey behaviors. If you make them rewarding enough, your dog will prefer to work with you and will be less inclined to chase prey. You can have him engage in activities which stimulate him and give him satisfaction while remaining a good friend to you and willing to live happily with you.

Physical exercise, when made rewarding, is another good alternative to chasing prey.

CHAPTER 6
TRAINING DEVICES AND METHODS TO AVOID

As mentioned at the beginning of the book, chase and prey behaviors are common among many breeds of dogs and are a difficult set of behaviors for the uninformed owner to deal with. Not surprisingly, a number of so-called experts have attempted to take advantage of this by recommending methods and devices that purport to try to solve this problem. Many are promoted as a "quick fix" or come with "guarantees." The more the product or method promises, the more skeptical you should be. Unfortunately, many of these products are based on a poor understanding of canine behavior and, in most cases, are not only ineffective but inhumane. Almost universally they depend on aversive methods that punish the dog.

Clearly, I am not a trainer who resorts to punishment to try to eradicate behaviors. Not only do I think it is not the right way to go, punishment is very difficult to administer in a way that will work, and in fact usually creates additional risks and problems for the dog. Permit me to insert some quotes from author Dorothée Schneider, a leading behaviorist and trainer of tracking dogs in Germany and author of *The World in His Head* (not available in the US) which help illustrate the risks and problems of using punishment:

> In order for the dog to be able to learn what is wanted from him after the punishment, a number of preconditions must be in place. Along with the respective strength of the stimuli, the chronological proximity of behavior to punishment in particular play a role. If a punisher is to be used in order to extinguish a particular behavior (for example, chasing game animals), the punisher must "reach the dog" at the moment in which he is about to start the chase. If he's already chasing the animal, then it is too late for a learning association to occur. Punishment that reaches the dog later than one second after the unwanted behavioral intention is pointless! The trainer does not have the possibility of *always* and *immediately* effecting punishment at the start of the unwanted behavior.

Also of concern is contextually related learning in dogs. Everything that the dog sees, smells, tastes, feels and hears at the moment of punishment is associated with the punisher and can later cause anxiety and stress to the dog! The trainer does not have the possibility of excluding unwanted secondary associations of the punishment with environmental stimuli. And, above all, he also does not have the possibility in the future of avoiding all environmental stimuli inadvertently associated with punishment.

If unwanted behavior is not always and immediately punished when it occurs, each unpunished performance of this behavior assumes a highly awarding character. So, if the dog manages to get away with it from time to time, for example, because the human was not paying attention at that moment because he was standing too far away from the dog, or because the electronic collar just didn't work properly, the dog will be variably rewarded for the (unwanted) behavior. The variable reward establishes behavior particularly firmly in the dog—this applies of course just as well to all unwanted behavioral traits. Complete monitoring of the dog in order to *always* and *immediately* be able to punish unwanted behavior is not possible for the trainer.

For punishment to also create the learning association that humans want, all(!) of the prerequisites listed above must be fulfilled—but one single one is! If we really look hard at the efficacy of punishers, the following pictures emerges:

In the normal daily environment, it is not possible to completely and continually fulfill all necessary prerequisites. If the unwanted behavior also involves strong motivation for the dog, then endorphins are released into the body. This chemical circulates in the blood, raises the pain threshold, and increases stamina. Endorphins are released during practically all instinctive behavior. The chemical is also built up in the body through all strongly drive-accentuated behaviors. The release of endorphins is an internal protective mechanism, which nevertheless provides for the stability of instinctive behavior, even under adverse conditions, and despite severe punishment. Instinctive behavior ensures the survival of a species. Additionally, there are the negative effects of stress that the dog endures against his will when he suffers or only suspects pain or fear. A dog is already exposed to a state of stress when he lives in expectation that what causes fear could happen—even when he is spared this in the future.

Devices to avoid

Electronic collars

Opinions are divided on the question of whether an electronic collar should be used during training with a dog who has

a strong prey drive. Even some trainers who use slogans such as "species-appropriate," "fair and friendly," or "without aversive methods," may promote the use of electronic collars including those that provide a shock to the dog—allegedly because nothing else works. The argument goes that while they are maybe not the "nicest" training tool, they provide the only means by which you can avoid prey behavior. You, the owner, just have to grin and bear it. You are told of all the terrible things that could happen to a dog if he races around out of control.

The use of electronic collars is morally unacceptable and can lead to serious health and psychological problems in the dog.

Unfortunately nobody describes what the dog will experience and suffer when exposed to this sort of "training." It does not change the fact that the dog is to be mistreated with electric shocks for engaging in instinctive, genetically pre-determined behavior.

Apart from the question of whether it is possible to control a dog's predatory behavior through punishment, you should first pause when someone recommends these training methods and ask yourself whether common sense and compassion for a living being entrusted to a human has not perhaps gotten lost. In my opinion, no one has the right to punish an animal for behavior that has been developed through evolutionary processes over thousands of years and is anchored in its genes—and electric shocks are nothing but punishment. Anyone who doubts this can try it out on himself! But, please, not at the lowest level on your arm or thigh—the device should be tightly strapped around your neck, with another person who has the remote control triggering the electric shock at middle to high level at exactly the moment when you show behavior that you consider normal!

Does this idea seem cruel or absurd to you? It is. Not only when it comes to humans, but also for dogs. Dogs are our companions, family members, and friends. For this reason, we should treat them with respect and esteem and do all that we can to keep them free of harm and suffering. It's that simple. Period!

Nevertheless, I would like to explain why shock collars should not be used even if you have no ethical qualms about using such a device. Dogs learn principally through association, that is, through a mental connection between two things that happen at the same time or within a very short time span. Shock collars are based on this concept. The idea is to get the dog to not engage in an unwanted predatory behavior because he supposedly will make a mental connection between the behavior and

the painful electric shocks. However, this idea carries with it incalculable risks.

No one can predict whether the dog, at the moment he receives *the* electric shock, will really make the mental association that the handler wants. A few years ago, for example, I was introduced to a dog who had been trained with a shock collar. He was just about to chase after a deer when the electric shock was triggered. At the same moment, a plane flew overhead. The dog connected the electric shock with the "thing in the sky." The result is a dog who still chases deer and panics at anything in the sky, whether it is a bird, a dark cloud that passes over the sun, a plane, or a hot air balloon. This association is so strong that he either tries to hide under a bush and refuses to move, or, when he is on an open, exposed field, he races to the car or back home and waits, quivering, for his owners. They are desperate and now wish that they had never used a shock collar.

The dog—and his owners—now have a serious problem in their daily lives which was not there before. At the same time, the original problem still hasn't been solved because the dog hunts just like he did before. Please consider that this "mis-association" could have happened with any event, object, or person! At the same moment he receives the electric shock, the dog sees an old man and is afraid of him, or all old men, from then on. Or, he sees a child who is just going past and associates him or her with the painful effect—there are thousands of possibilities that cannot be calculated in advance.

In the study, *Basic Principles of Dog Training in Accordance with Animal Welfare,* published in 1998 by the German Dog Society, it was clearly documented that the behavior of animals after using electric shock collars clearly differs from their previous behavior:

> All dogs (in the study) were impaired in their social behavior toward their owner. With the exception of one animal, all of them behaved fearfully, were frantic, didn't stay near the owner, and avoided him constantly. A Rottweiler that, before stimulation with the shock collar, was conspicuous in his self-assuredness and

impressiveness, and who could be stopped (by other means) as he was about to run off, appeared in the next test run just as confident as before, but seemed agitated and threatened the tester directly. A Giant Schnauzer was not responsive, cowered whimpering in the corner, and demonstrated apathy. The self-assuredness in most of the dogs was also suppressed, they avoided the stimuli they encountered without fear in the first run, crouched with a cowering posture, or moved around and demonstrated defecation distress. A Dachshund ran in panic in a zig-zag across the ground, demonstrated pronounced flight behavior and ran/jumped into the fence.

In other words, the claim by the supporters of electric shock collars that the treatment is not really so bad for the dog and that he would not associate what he experiences with the owner is completely and utterly untrue.

The question is now raised of whether the companies that make shock collars and the trainers who use these devices deliberately withhold this information from the dog owners, or whether they have so little professional competence that they really do not know what they are doing. And the question is also raised as to which of the two is worse!

Ultimately, it is a question of trust. I want my dog to trust me and for him to be sure at all times that I will respect him, protect him, and treat him fairly. I am convinced that mutual trust is the basis for good cooperation and bonding. To me, trust from the dog's perspective means being willing to risk that his owner will be consistent and reliable in his reactions and behaviors. Trust means being able to expect that the other has your best interests at heart.

I do not want to lose or jeopardize in any way the trust of my dogs or the dogs entrusted to me as a trainer. It goes without saying that this completely rules out the use of electric shock collars or other fear and/or pain triggering stimuli. How could I do such a terrible thing to a (or my) dog?

Lithium salts

The use of lithium salts was developed as a method to prevent wolves from attacking sheep by the American Wildlife Project. Wolf attacks on sheep were leading to considerable problems with ranchers, most of who were already skeptical and bitterly opposed to wolf repopulation projects. Lithium salts were laid out on pieces of sheep which the wolves eventually would find and eat. Lithium causes copious vomiting that can last for days. Additionally, the animal suffers from diarrhea and an extreme sensation of thirst. The desired learning association was that the wolf would learn to avoid mutton (that is, the sheep) in the future because the food was inedible and led to considerable discomfort.

The problem with this is that the vomiting that is caused can lead to an old, weak, or sick animal not surviving at all, or with considerable damage to health. Additionally, a high dose (which was recommended) can lead to cardiac arrhythmia, changes in the EKG, kidney damage, and cerebral seizures!

I do not want to pass judgment on whether these drastic deterrent measures are justifiable or right as it relates to the reintroduction of the wolf into his original habitat. But, for our pet dogs, it is most certainly not. And the practice of using lithium salts on a wide variety of prey animals such as hares, deer, squirrels, cats, and so on would be dangerous and impractical. Despite all of this, this method is recommended again and again. One can only assume that the trainer who does this is just simply not adequately aware of the risks.

Weighted saddlebags

It is sometimes recommended that a dog wear weighted saddlebags because then his willingness to run quickly, let alone chase, will be reduced. Experience shows that that is not the case. The sight of a deer or a crisscrossing hare makes many dogs run off—along with the saddlebag flapping wildly around him.

Another problem is that when these bags are unbalanced or too heavily packed, the dog can develop serious back problems.

If the bags are not well padded, pressure sores can occur—particularly in the sensitive spinal region.

Chaining the dog to a heavy object

Yes, this advice is also given from time to time. An example is attaching a field leash or chain to a heavy tire to limit a dog's mobility. The idea is similar to that of the weighted saddlebag. Because of the heavy weight of the tire or similar object and the energy expended by the dog in order to drag it behind him, he loses the desire for strenuous hunting and chasing—but also for walking. In anxious dogs, with such a large, heavy thing attached to them, rumbling behind them, it can also lead to panic attacks.

Spray collars

This really is just a "gentle version" of an electric shock collar. The dog wears a collar with a receiver around his neck and the human carries a trigger mechanism in his hand. When the collar is correctly positioned, the moment the trigger is pressed, a short blast of citronella or air from below hits the dog's muzzle. The idea is that a startle effect will become associated with the unwanted behavior and therefore the dog will stop doing it. It gives the dog owner the chance to introduce a desired alternative behavior by, for example, a successful recall. The theory is good. The reality is unfortunately different. Generally, three reactions to these types of devices are observed in the dog:

1. The dog is surprised, stands still, and then reacts to the owner's call. The problem is that often, after two to five times, he is no longer surprised and continues running.

2. It causes no reaction at all in the dog and he continues running.

3. The dog is very sensitive and is so frightened by the blast of air or spray that he actually stops the behavior. The problem is that, in general, a sensitive dog is not just impacted by this incident, but also frightened. Similar problems during its use can arise in the same way as with the use of the electric shock collar.

In addition to this, these devices are often unreliable. Sometimes, there is a time lag in the release of the blast of air, sometimes it doesn't come at all. During wet weather or on hilly terrain, the technology frequently fails. Unfortunately, it can also be triggered by other transmitters in the immediate vicinity. So, if you are walking through the park with your dog and someone else nearby triggers a device for his own dog, your dog could also get a blast—without having shown any unwanted behavior.

Training methods and activities to avoid

Life on a leash or field leash
When used correctly, both the normal leash and the field leash are practical tools and can be used in the process of developing solid off-leash recalls (see Chapter 4). However, even when properly used, there are some dogs whose prey drive is so deeply ingrained that it will either take a very long time before any success in training can be achieved or—in extreme cases—it will never happen. So in many cases, attempts at off-leash training are abandoned much too soon and the dog is then kept on the leash for life. The dog never gets to enjoy just "being a dog," free to explore on his own.

Hiding from your dog games
"If your dog is not paying attention, hide and let yourself be seen only when he is really scared." How many times have I heard this dubious tip? Let's examine more closely what might result if you hide when your dog is not paying attention, or maybe is off hunting somewhere. Let's assume you go for walks with a dog with a normal prey drive. You hide at a moment when he is not paying attention to you.

Result A. You have a self confident, adult dog who starts to search for you and, thanks to the capabilities of his nose, soon finds you. He has learned that, from time to time, we play this nice hiding game, and my human is always happy when I find him. This has no effect on his predatory behavior.

Result B. You have a very self confident, adult dog who doesn't care how long you continue to hide because you have played

This type of hiding game is not a good idea. "Playing" with your dog's fear of being abandoned is not a suitable, and certainly not fair, exercise.

this "game" so often that he is fed up with it. As far as he cares, you can take root while he is off indulging his passion for hunting until he meets up with you at your car or home. By the way, that doesn't necessarily mean (as is often maintained) that your dog has a weak bond with you. It may well be that he greets you with the utmost joy when you finally meet up. In the evening, he will cuddle up to you blissfully when he dreams, his paws twitching, yelping and woofing away about his adventures today.

Result C. You have a very insecure, possibly even anxious dog. When you hide, he learns that "I must keep an eye out for my human or else he will run away and I will be alone." Your dog's already not very well developed self-confidence will be dealt another blow. He will soon start to follow your every footstep in the constant fear of otherwise being abandoned by you. If you come to believe that that is good because then he won't run away anymore, you should be aware of the side effects. Your dog will become increasingly more psychologically dependent on you. It may reach the point that you can hardly go to the bathroom alone, or your dog might develop separation anxiety when you want to leave him alone at home.

You should on no account play this hiding game with a puppy! I am always appalled when I hear this recommended. Your puppy should trust you, should be able to count on you being there for him, caring for him, and being his "port in the storm" when danger threatens. Instead of this, you would be playing with his fear of abandonment.

Imagine the following situation: A group of mothers are sitting on a bench in a playground, their one to three-year-old children are playing in the sand. They are totally absorbed in creating new shapes in the sand, discovering a fantasy world in which they are completely immersed and forget everything around them. The one mother says to another, "You know, your child is not paying attention to you. Hide quickly and then see what he does when he notices you are not here." The mother then walks off unnoticed and hides behind a large tree. Eventually, after a certain time, the child notices that his mother isn't there any more. At first, he looks in astonishment around him and searches with his small eyes for the trusted form of the most important person in his world. After a few moments, astonishment gives way to anxiety, the child starts to call out, cry, and run around calling for his mommy. The mother jumps from behind the tree and has a great laugh about it with the other women about how sweet the little tyke looked when he was searching for his mother.

Do you find this scenario appalling? Would you wonder how anyone could do such a gruesome and stupid thing? Yes, I feel the same. And the same applies to dog children as well.

With such behavior, you neither create trust nor a bond but fear and mistrust—conceivably, bad preconditions for cooperation.

Constant activity and interaction

Another idea I hear frequently is to keep your dog permanently busy and distracted so that he has absolutely no time to search for tracks or otherwise to just "be a dog." In general, it may be a good idea to do things together with your dog during a walk (see Chapter 3), but if you overdo it, the result is not necessarily a very enthusiastic or obedient dog, but rather an incredibly stressed one. Eventually, the dog may stay away from you because he wants to have peace and quiet.

During a guided hiking tour with dogs in a Bavarian forest I saw a great example of this. A young woman, who was taking part in the hike with a dog with an obviously high prey drive, was trying to control the dog with instructions. It went like this:

"Benny, no!" (The dog was sniffing at the side of the path.)

"Benny, fine!" (The dog had stopped sniffing on the edge of the path.)

"Benny, no!" (Benny looked towards the forest.)

"Benny, fine!" (Benny had stopped looking towards the forest.)

"Benny, fetch a stick. Go look for a little stick. A little stick. Quickly."

"I have to keep Benny busy or he runs off." (She said by way of explanation to the woman who was walking next to her.)

"Benny, nooooo!" (Benny wanted to run on to a field where a few dogs were running around, while his owner thought he wanted to go hunting.)

"Oh, Benny, it's ok. Mommy's mistake. Just go on and play." (She said when she noticed her mistake.)

"Benny, fine!" (She said when he came back from playing and…)

"Benny, no!" (When he again looked towards the thicket around us.)

And so it went on for more than an hour until one of the hikers said he would ring her neck if he heard "Benny, no!" or "Benny, fine!" one more time. When the dog then finally shot off on a wild hunt we were all in agreement that it was probably done out of pure desperation in order to get away on his own.

When I asked her why she was going on a hike through one of the most heavily populated game areas in Europe with this highly prey driven dog, she said that was the reason she was going. She wanted to practice with her dog. I told her to consider the fact that she was demanding high school graduation before the dog had finished elementary school. She couldn't even let him run free in a city park, where there were only a few rabbits—without him shooting off.

It seemed to make sense to her, but at the same time she didn't have a clue about how to deal with the situation and asked me what I would do if I were in her shoes. I advised her to leave, which she in fact did the next day. Without a doubt the right decision, because she was very unhappy, stressed, overwhelmed, and was becoming increasingly impatient with the dog.

Lure coursing

If you have a sight hound, you may have been advised to let him engage in lure coursing or running on a racetrack. If your ultimate goal is to allow your dog to run free (at least occasionally) during walks, then I can only advise you against lure coursing. On a course, the dog chases after a mechanical hare that usually consists of real fur. How will the dog understand that he is allowed to chase after this hare but not the others out in the wild?

Lure coursing in action.

Consider also the high release of adrenaline during the chase. Your dog will probably become extremely excited and obsessed with prey and you will have considerable problems keeping him under control during walks, assuming this is at all possible.

Attempting to extinguish prey drive

Research speaks of extinguishing behavior so that something previously learned by the dog is discontinued. This can often be achieved if you can alter things so that the behavior in question no longer benefits the dog.

Here's a common example. A dog begs at the table when the family sits down to dinner. This strategy is mostly successful because sooner or later usually he gets something. Then the family resolves to solve this annoying problem and so the dog is no longer to be fed at the table. If this agreement is adhered to in painstaking detail and at all times, he will eventually stop begging. He has learned that his previous successful behavioral strategy is now unsuccessful and pointless. Therefore, the behavior is discontinued and the dog doesn't beg at the table anymore. In other words, it is extinguished.

This strategy, however, does not work well with predatory be-havior because, as previously stated, you are dealing with in-stinctive, genetically predetermined behavior. It is almost im-possible to extinguish, unlike the begging behavior mentioned above. As the trigger for this behavior (sight of game animals, tracks/scents, or noises) cannot *always* be avoided, the dog will occasionally be "successful" in engaging in this behavior even if he only pursues the prey for a short distance. And since that short sprint is usually found very reinforcing, it makes it almost impossible to set up the no-more-chance-of-success pattern that is vital to extinguishing a behavior.

Using an adaptation strategy

In adaptation, we assume that a stimulus loses meaning because it neither brings benefits nor disadvantages. For example, a family with a Cocker Spaniel moves into a house that is near a train track. When the dog is lying in the garden, a train goes by. The dog is frightened by the noise created by the train because he is not accustomed to it. Over time, as more and more trains go by he learns to cope with the noise. Within a few days, the dog snoozes quietly away on the terrace, completely unaffected by the noise of the trains. He has now learned that trains going by have no consequence for him. He has become used to the noise and doesn't react to it anymore.

The question of whether it is possible to use an adaptation strategy with a dog by frequently/constantly getting him to observe game animals so that he no longer reacts to them is not at all easy to answer with "yes" or "no." Anders Hallgren recommends that you try to accustom a dog to sight prey by attaching a toy animal to a string and then tossing it ahead of the dog. At the same time, train him to remain still in spite of the distraction. On the surface, this is a practical and logical proposal.

While this strategy might work to some degree, it may not work consistently. That is because predatory behavior is not about *acquired* key stimuli, but about *innate* trigger mechanisms. That means that even just the sight of the prey may set the entire behavioral chain in motion, and this is again self-rewarding. For this reason, training through adaptation is not likely to work over time.

Using avoidance tactics exclusively

To a certain extent, it makes sense to use avoidance tactics. If I have a dog with a high prey drive, I will not, for example, go for a walk in the morning through a forest where the dew-fresh tracks of wild animals can be found. If my dog chases a neighbor's cat, I will not take him with me to visit a friend who has three cats running around in the garden, and so on.

However, you will reach the limit of what you can do very quickly. There is hardly any place where some trigger factor is not to be found—the squirrels in the city park, the rabbits on a nearby farm, the bicyclists in the neighborhood, the birds in the fields, etc.

Also, remember you will not always spot "prey" before your dog, especially when you consider a dog's sensory abilities. At least in regards to prey, we see worse, we hear worse, we react more slowly, and our sense of smell is not at all comparable.

In other words, you should use avoidance tactics whenever possible. But all too often it will prove to be impossible to do so.

Having the "victim" defend himself

If you have a dog who chases cats, small animals, deer, or other animals, you have probably been given the advice to confront him with a "real alley cat," a sullen billy goat, or a feisty goose. Such recommendations are based on the idea that the dog will think twice about attacking such an animal in the future, and his motivation to go near this type of animal will decrease greatly if he is attacked by such an animal and gets a really good beating.

Apart from the fact that I find it morally difficult to support the idea of deliberately setting two living beings upon each other at the risk of both being seriously injured, one doesn't know how bad the injuries inflicted on the animals may be. Here are a few examples from recent years that clearly illustrate what I mean:

Jacko, a Golden Retriever, who was a passionate cat chaser, cornered the neighbor's tomcat one day. Both animals faced each other ready to fight and Jacko's owner could have easily taken the opportunity to pull him back. The neighbor was of the opinion, however, that his tomcat could fend for himself and Jacko should get what's coming to him. In the future, he would give all cats a wide berth. His owner found this prospect so enticing that she actually allowed it to come to a fight. As the animals attacked each other, growling and snarling, the owner could sense that this was not such a good idea after all. The fighting noises did not sound good and neither of the two wanted to concede. Then she heard her dog wince loudly and decided to separate the two. Both had wounds inflicted upon them. The tomcat had "only" suffered some shock and a few scratches. Jacko had been particularly badly injured in the facial area—he lost an eye that could not be saved despite intense veterinary intervention. Jacko's owner says today that she is really ashamed of her behavior and her stupidity. The owner of the tomcat says that nobody could have predicted it would end so badly. Jacko hates cats more than ever and still tries to catch one at every opportunity.

Betty, a German Shorthair, had a similar encounter to Jacko. When she was five years old she was confronted with a tomcat that, with his back to the stall wall, was hissing dangerously at her. Likewise, the owners were of the opinion the two should have it out between them—an adult tomcat knows how to look after himself, and Betty should be taught a good lesson and then she would leave cats in peace in the future. Betty got a few scratches during the ensuing fight—and killed the cat.

The owners of Freddy, a Great Dane mix, also kept three ponies in a small paddock adjoining the house. During the day, the small horses would run around in the very large garden and would regularly chase the young dog across the garden, and even lash out at him. The owners told me, amused, that the small pony stallion was downright fixated on Freddy, and would corner him and then chase him wildly across the garden. Occasionally, he received a kick or a small bite, but nothing serious. Freddy would always flee in panic as soon as one of the ponies came near, which they thought was good because he would then learn to respect them and to stay out of their way. I warned them urgently about letting things run their course. I explained to them that their dog could really get seriously injured if he couldn't dodge one of the targeted kicks quickly enough. The following weeks and months showed that they hadn't taken my warnings seriously, but the result was different from what I had feared.

Freddy grew to a stately size and had enormous power. When we met while going for walks I took care to ensure his greetings and declarations of love didn't end up with me getting bruised. At the age of fourteen months, he was almost as large as a Dane but considerably more powerful, and I joked with friends that Freddy had to be a mix of Dane and elephant—there was no other explanation for his powerful stature. He had a friendly character, was well socialized with his fellow dogs and humans, sometimes a little too boisterous (typical for the age), but otherwise well trained—and still fled in panic from the ponies when they ran around free in the garden.

When Freddy was one and a half years old he must have decided that it was now time to defend himself. When his owner came into the kitchen in the morning, he discovered blood traces on the dog and on the floor. Shaken, he checked Freddy but couldn't find any injury. He could find no explanation for the situation and, in order to see some sign of a fight or something similar, looked outside through the terrace door, which was open in summer. He presumed that maybe Freddy had run a burglar off or killed a marten—but he couldn't find solid evidence for these theories. Because the dog was okay, he first made coffee and went to the stall to let the ponies out. The sight that greeted him resembled a butcher's store. The pony stallion and the older mare were dead. They lay in a pool of their own blood; their throats and bellies torn out, and had countless other injuries. The younger mare, the daughter of the two, stood in a corner of the stall completely distraught, with several serious bite wounds. After the vet had seen to her, the telephone in my dog school rang. In a fluster, the owners told me the entire story and, when I asked them how they reacted to the situation, they told me they had dragged Freddy to the stall, shown him what he had done and then really gave him a good lashing with the leash. They were absolutely disgusted by his behavior and didn't want to keep him anymore. If they kept him, every time they looked at him, they would be reminded of the ponies lying in their own blood. They asked me to come and get Freddy today. If I found a new home for him with other people, I should tell the truth about the dog's killer instinct.

I drove immediately to the house and fetched Freddy. He was distraught, but otherwise as friendly as ever, and jumped without a fuss into my automobile. His owners cried the entire time, but refused to say goodbye to him or to think things over one more time. I suggested they were not exactly innocent in the dramatic end to the story between the ponies and the dog— which they just didn't want to see. A few weeks later, I found Freddy a lovely home with really nice people who have been living with their "calf" (endearing pet name for Freddy) for years now. He is a very nice dog who gets along very well with all humans and also with his fellow dogs and other animals. Only ponies and horses are a "no go area." He gives them a wide berth and makes sure he gets away as quickly as possible.

Shooting dogs with an air rifle

I think this is the most unbelievable tip for what to do with a dog whose prey drive could not be controlled using an electric shock collar. Erik Zimen, an otherwise noted researcher, recommends a targeted shot at the dog with an air rifle. He wrote:

> For a long time, the dogs' urge for freedom was not dampened by this [the use of the electric shock collar]. When it came back once again, a friend and good dog handler recommended the air rifle. Quiet, unerring, and from a distance of 150 feet totally safe, it would work real wonders. Test shots on a wooden plank showed that he was right about it with regard to possible injuries if you kept to the distance. And the first strike in the hind parts of Raas, who had been provoked into running away by my deliberate lack of attention, was a thorough success. For a few weeks there has been peace. I always carry the

air rifle with me when I am on the farm with the dogs. And, as long as I carry the weapon, they stay close to me. Even when I hide it in the hay without the dogs noticing, they don't run away. I can muck out the stalls, speak to the horses, give them hay, and behave as if I had fully forgotten the dogs were there. Raas and Pfiff seem to know exactly that I have this weapon nearby, and if it goes bang, they'll feel a stinging pain in their backsides.

For anyone who doesn't know about weapons, air rifles are used for shooting birds. The injuries generally result in the death of the animal. A weapons dealer in a specialist shop for hunting equipment where I enquired explained that shooting at a dog could indeed result in an injury that would need veterinary treatment. He also said I could rest assured, because no sensible and responsible person would ever do such a thing.

As the following example illustrates, apart from the gunshot wound, it can also lead to mental associations that put psychological strain on the dog and cause him considerable problems in his daily life. At the age of two, the dog of a friend of mine was accidentally shot with an air rifle and slightly hurt. The wound was treated and healed quickly. Since this experience, however, the dog has developed a terrible fear of shots, which has generalized into a fear of other bangs or loud noises. Despite intensive training, the now ten-year old dog still carries this fear with him!

It may be to Zimen's credit that he wanted to control his dogs' prey drive out of fear for their safety (according to his account, they had been shot at by other hunters and had dragged themselves back home injured), but it still has to be stated clearly that such tips overstep the boundaries of animal welfare.

THE STORY OF FENGARI

I recently met a dog whose prey drive I knew, right after our first walk together, would never be really brought under control. I like to tell this story because you may own or encounter a dog whose drives are so strong that no matter what you do or how you train, you may never be able to overcome his desire to chase prey. He may always have to be on a field leash if you want to insure his safety.

Fengari was a mixed-breed dog who belonged to a colleague of mine. We went for a walk along the bank of the river. My own dogs, two of whom have a prey drive that could be classified as very strong, were also with us and were running free. Fengari was on a thirty-foot long field leash. The area in which we were walking was "safe" because there are practically no game animals on our side of the bank, and the fairly wide, fast-flowing river along which we were walking separated us from the game area. We were confident that no dog would be crazy enough to throw himself into the torrent and, because Fengari looked with such longing at my dogs playing with each other on the bank of the river, we decided to let her run free. Where could she go, she just wanted to play with the others and she should be allowed her fun, right?

What then followed taught us to know better. Without hesitating for one second, Fengari raced the few feet to the river, jumped into the water, and gracefully started to swimming across the river. Halfway across the river she began struggling against the current, her strength ebbed, and she let herself be carried downstream. Finally, she reached the other bank around 500 feet diagonally from us and, in a flash, ran across the field and disappeared into the adjoining forest. I have to admit that I was speechless. My feelings swayed between unfettered admiration for the capabilities of this dog (she would definitely survive if she were ever released into the wild!), worry that something could happen to her, and disbelief at our own misjudgment. My colleague shrugged her shoulders and said: "I told you that she had a very strong prey drive. I'm sure she'll come back. We'll just have to wait a bit."

After around 25 minutes, she appeared on the opposite river-bank. I started to think about how we could get her back over to our side again. She had obviously been running around the whole time and was exhausted. She would surely not be able to make it across the river a second time. Then, while I was considering fetching my automobile and driving the three miles to the bridge in order to collect her, Fengari sprang without hesitation into the river, applied the same swimming and drifting technique, climbed over the bushes, and ran enthusiastically to us.

When she reached us, I noticed something that I hadn't seen before. Fengari's face wasn't just beaming—her eye color had changed. Her look was frantic and wild; the color of her eyes was a lucid yellowy-amber color. She seemed ecstatic about her trip although she had apparently not caught any prey. She wouldn't have had enough time and she didn't have any blood on her. But she had tasted freedom and for almost half an hour she had surrendered herself to her drive and had simply followed her instinct.

Her owner also noticed it and we both had the same thought— was it at right for this dog to live a strictly regulated life in an industrialized country in the middle of Europe? Could anyone ever satisfy her urge for freedom, her ingrained instinct? Should we deny this dog the opportunity to engage in this activity? We discussed this issue and it was clear to us that we ultimately wouldn't find any answers. And another thing was clear to us— Fengari would stay on the field leash in the future! Even though, deep down, it made us sad.

CLOSING THOUGHTS

Always remember that your dog has been entrusted to you, you are responsible for his well being. Far too many people believe that unwanted predatory behavior justifies the use of all manner of methods, some nonsensical, others somewhere between brutal and downright cruel, because they have not found that any other training methods work. Of course, these arguments come from those who have not tried anything else apart from pain, fright, or lifelong leading on the leash.

Never let anyone talk you into accepting that there is a justification for subjecting your dog to pain and/or fear, especially when trying to deal with an instinctive behavior. If such training is presented to you, always ask yourself whether you would like to be treated in such a way if you were a dog. If you cannot answer this question with a definite "yes", then don't do it. If devices are presented to you, test them on yourself if you are not sure whether they are really harmless as described by the manufacturer or user. If you get a very bad feeling by the mere thought of it, you should not allow it to be used on your dog.

I have been working with the training program presented in this book for many years and have continually revised and amended it. I would like to encourage you with all my heart to try it out. It abstains from the use of aversive stimuli and generally leads to the desired success. Many owners who thought nothing more could be done to solve their dog's prey behaviors, are now able to allow their dog to be off-leash safely.

It demands patience, perseverance and consistency, empathy, a good ability to observe and the willingness to learn about dogs and their breed-specific behavior. Your reward for the effort you invest will be a better understanding of your dog and even more togetherness.

Soon, you will be able to see the first successes. Be prepared for setbacks as well ingrained prey behaviors do not disappear over night. Do not despair, but rather search for the source of error with the help of the training diary you keep, and work on solving the problem. Training never stops, and so for this reason alone you should organize it in such a way that is fun for both you and your dog.

When the first success comes, and your dog prefers to go with you rather than pursue prey, it is probably the greatest present that he can give you. This makes all the effort worthwhile. These are the golden moments of deep solidarity in my life together with my dogs.

I wish you and your dog much success and, above all, have a wonderful time training.

THANKS

I would like thank all dogs, from whom I have learned so much. Most of the ideas and elements of the training program described in this book came through observing and working with them. Particularly noteworthy are:

- Debbie, whose passion for hunting waterfowl drove me to the point of distraction until she eventually let herself be recalled—what a moment of joy and triumph after weeks of grueling training, full of doubt about whether I was on the right track with this program.

- Chenook, who came to me at the age of two and a half with a very strong prey drive and today prefers my company to that of the deer and hares—what a testament to friendship!

- Shorty, a mix of Chihuahua and Shiba Inu, a real rascal, who taught me that this training is never over. For weeks it went perfectly—and then he shot off into the forest and resurfaced fifteen minutes later, making me humbly realize that we still had training to do. Then it was okay for a few weeks—or even months. He made me increasingly better at recognizing the signs for the right moment to do follow-up training.

- Jule, also a loyal companion, who gave me the idea for the sausage tree.

- Fengari, who deeply impressed me with her behavior and made me rethink how far we can, and ought to, interfere with the instinctive behavior of our domestic dogs.

- Elsa, who has accompanied me since her youth and doesn't waste a single thought on deer or other prey animals when we are out walking together.

FURTHER READING

Bones Would Rain from the Sky. On Deepening our Relationships with Dogs, Suzanne Clothier. Warner, 2005.

Dogs. A New Understanding of Canine Origin, Behavior, and Evolution, Ray and Lorna Coppinger. Schibner, 2001.

On Talking Terms with Dogs, Calming Signals, 2nd Ed. Turid Rugaas. Dogwise Publishing, 2006.

Stress in Dogs, Learn How Dogs Show Stress and What You Can Do to Help, Martina Scholz and Clarissa von Reinhardt. Dogwise Publishing, 2006.

INDEX

A

abandonment, 104–107
activities
  alignment exercises, 64–65
  communicative walks and, 39–44
  to enhance owner concentration, 46–47
  mental activities, 92–93
  methods to avoid, 104–115
  physical activities, 94
  playing. See play activities
  for recall, 59–63
adaptation strategies, 110
adrenaline, 10, 78–79, 109
aggression, prey
  attempts to extinguish, 109–110
  play activities and, 78–79
  in terriers, 12
air rifles, 114–115
alignment exercises, 64–65
American Wildlife Project, 102
anticipation of dogs' behavior, 24–25
anxiety, 97, 106. See also stress related problems
area search, 91
attacks by other animals, 111–114
attitudes of owners, effects on training, 51–52, 68, 76

B

automatic sitting behavior, 72–74
avoidance tactics, 111

balancing activities, 81, 94
Basic Principles of Dog Training in Accordance with Animal Welfare (German Dog Society), 100–101
Beagles, 13–14
body language
  of dogs, 2, 14–17, 69
  effects on training, 59, 75
  of trainer, 23, 52
Border Collies, 12
Borzois, 13
breed disposition, 11–14

C

cancer cell detection, 92
cats, 25, 111–112
chains, 103
challenges for dogs, 92–93
change of direction behavior, 65–67
chase behavior, explained, 1–2
chase behavior patterns, 4–7
cigarettes, 76
citronella, 103
Cocker Spaniels, 13
collars

electronic devices in, 1,
97–101, 114
spray devices in, 103–104
use with field leash, 35
come commands, 59–62
commands
change of direction behavior,
65–67
come, 59–62
down at a distance, 58
"look here", 59–61
"psst", 24, 62
remaining on the path behavior, 69–70
sit at a distance, 56–58, 72–74
sit behavior, 49–50, 52–61,
72–74
slowing down behavior, 69–71
stay behavior, 49–50, 52–61
"this way", 50, 65–67
"to me", 59–61
"turn around", 50, 59–61
communication
activities for enhancing, 37–47
body language. See body
language
leashes and, 31–32
tactile contact, 40–41
visual, 39–40
communicative walks, 37–47
concentration exercises for
owner, 46–47
confidence of owner, 76
contextually related learning, 97
cuddling, 40–41

D

Dachshunds, 13
defense tactics, 111–114
devices to avoid, 98–103, 119
digging activities, 86–87
direction, changing, 65–67

diseases, effects on training, 49,
63, 75
distractions, 29–30, 49, 54–55
dog fishing rod, 79–80
down behavior, 49–50, 58
drug identification, 92

E

electronic collars, 1, 97–101, 114
electronic fences, 1
elements of training, 22–29
endorphins, 97–98
environment
communicative walks and,
45–47
relationship to punishment,
97
equipment for training, 30–35
exercises
alignment, 64–65
communicative walks and,
39–44
to enhance owner concentration, 46–47
mental activities, 92–93
methods to avoid, 104–115
physical activities, 94
play activities. See play activities
for recall, 59–63
explosive detection, 92
expressive behavior of dogs,
14–17
eye contact
activities involving, 39–40
alignment exercises and, 64
as means of communication,
38
sight of prey and, 72–73
sit command and, 59
eye stalking, 4–5, 14

F

failure, sources of. See problems in training
Fengari, story of, 116–118
field leashes, 32–35, 104
fights between animals, 111–114
finding objects activities, 82–85, 88–91
fishing rod, 79–80
food as rewards in training. See treats
frequency of commands, problems with, 74
fundamentals of training, 22–29

G

games
    activities to avoid, 78–80
    benefits of, 80–81, 94
    digging activities, 86–87
    hidden treats activities, 41–44, 82–85
    hiding from dog, 104–107
    nose work, 88–92
    problem solving, 92–93
gardens, digging in, 86–87
German Dog Society, 100–101
Greyhounds, 13–14
guns, 114–115

H

Hallgren, Anders, 93, 110
harnesses, 30, 35
health problems. See also stress related problems
    effects on training, 49, 63, 75
    electronic collars and, 98–101
    lithium salts and, 102
    weighted saddlebags and, 102–103
hearing, sense of, 15
"heel" command, 69

herding dogs, 11
hidden treats activities, 41–44, 82–85
hip dysplasia, 63
hormones
    adrenaline, 10, 78–79, 109
    endorphins, 97–98
horses, 112–114
hunger, 18–20
hunting
    breed disposition for, 12–14
    hunger as motivation, 18–20
    strategies, 8–10
    training for, 79–80
Huskies, 12

I

infection of the anal glands, 63

K

killing strategies, 9–10

L

Labradors, 14
learning games, 92–93
leashes, 30–35, 104
lithium salts, 102
"look here" command, 59–61
lure coursing, 108–109

M

management of dogs' behavior, 25
mechanical hare, 108–109
Mental Activation, Ways to Stimulate Your Dog's Brain and Avoid Boredom (Hallgren), 93
methods to avoid, 104–115
mixed breeds, 14
mood transfer, 5, 32, 51–52, 68
mother dogs, influence of, 5–7
movement behaviors, 50

N

nudging, 40–41

O

obedience and physical exercise, 94
observing dog's behavior, 16
obstacle course, 94
orientation posture, 8

P

pack behavior, 7–8
path, remaining on, 69–70
petting, 40–41
physical exercise, 94
physical problems
    effects on training, 63, 75
    electronic collars and, 98–101
    lithium salts and, 102
    weighted saddlebags and, 102–103
play activities
    benefits of, 80–81, 94
    digging activities, 86–87
    games to avoid, 78–80, 104–107
    hidden treats, 41–44, 82–85
    nose work, 88–92
    overview of appropriate games, 80–81
    problem solving games, 92–93
Pointers, 11, 13
pointing, 9
poisons, 102
positive mood transfer, 51–52, 68
posture
    of dogs, 14–17, 69
    effects on training, 59, 75
    of trainer, 23, 52
predatory behavior
    explained, 1–2

killing strategies, 9–10
patterns of, 4–7
sequence of, 8
predatory games, 78–80
prey aggression
    attempts to extinguish, 109–110
    play activities and, 78–79
    in terriers, 12
problem solving games, 92–93
problems in training
    hiding from dog, 67
    recall exercises and, 63–64
    sources of, 74–76, 98–103, 104–115
"psst" command, 24, 62
punishment
    devices to avoid, 98–103, 119
    effects on training, 51–52
    methods to avoid, 104–115
    reasons to avoid, 2, 96–97, 119

R

recall training behaviors, 59–63
record keeping, 22
remaining on the path behavior, 69–70
rest behaviors, 50
Retrievers, 11, 13, 87
retrieving, 78–80
rewards. See also treats
    proper use in training, 25–29, 83–86
    sausage trees, 41–44
rifles, air, 114–115

S

saddlebags, weighted, 102–103
sand boxes, 86–87
sausage trees, 41–44
Schneider, Dorothée, 96–98
search and rescue, 88–91
seeing, sense of, 15

self-rewarding action, 10
senses of dogs, 15–17, 88–92
separation anxiety, 106
sequence of predatory behavior, 8
Setters, 13–14
shock collars, 1, 97–101, 114
Sight hounds, 108–109
sit at a distance, 56–58, 72–74
sit behavior, 49–50, 52–61, 72–74
slowing down behavior, 69–71
smell, sense of, 15–16, 88–92
Spondylosis, 63
spray collars, 103–104
stalking, 4, 7, 8. See also hunting; tracking
staring behavior, 4–5
stay behavior, 49–50, 52–61
stimulus control, 90
stress related problems. See also anxiety
    activities to avoid, 79, 107–108
    air rifles and, 114–115
    punishment and, 97–103
stroking, 40–41
substance identification, 88, 92

T
tactile contact, 38, 40–41
tail posture, 16
Terriers, 13–14, 87
The World in His Head (Schneider), 96–98
"this way" command, 50, 51, 65–67
timing, communicative walks and, 45–47
"to me" command, 59–61
tone of voice, 24, 52, 59. See also attitudes of owners, effects on training

touching, communicating by, 38, 40–41
toys, 75, 78–80, 90
tracking, 15, 45–46, 88–90
training
    commands and. See commands
    communicative walks and, 37–47
    devices to avoid, 98–103
    equipment for, 30–35
    fundamentals of, 22–29
    importance of positive attitude, 51–52, 68, 76
    methods to avoid, 104–115
    punishment and, 96–97
    recall exercises, 59–63
training diary, 22
treats
    problems with, 75
    as rewards in training, 25–29
    sausage trees, 41–44
    use of in games, 79, 82–87, 93
turn around behavior, 50, 67–69

V
vocal signals. See also attitudes of owners, effects on training
    tone of voice, 24, 52, 59
    understanding of dogs, 38–39
volume of sound, 24

W
walks, communicating and, 37–47
weather, effects on training, 49, 52, 59, 75
weighted saddlebags, 102–103
wolves, 8, 102

Z
Zimen, Erik, 114–115

ABOUT THE AUTHOR

Clarissa v. Reinhardt has lived and worked with dogs for more than twenty years. In 1993, she founded her own dog school, Animal Learn. She chose the name as a play on words that can be taken in three ways: animals learn, learning about animals, and learning from animals. And that's exactly what she wanted to achieve—cooperation in life based on trust and joint learning.

In 1994, she founded a seminar center that holds 20—30 seminars for cynological experts every year. The highlight is the annual International Dog Symposium, to which speakers from the around the world travel and which offers the perfect platform for further training and exchange between colleagues.

In 1995, she started a training course for dog trainers that has since become very popular. The students are trained intensively for one and a half years and prepared for a career as dog trainers. After successfully passing the final examination, they carry the concept of nonviolent training to their own dog schools, or into their work in animal welfare.

In 2000, she founded the publishing house, *Animal Learn Verlag*, which specializes extensively in cynological expert literature and enjoys great popularity in all of the German speaking countries. It serves as a guarantee for worldwide renowned and highly qualified authors such as Turid Rugaas, Prof. Ray Coppinger, James O'Heare, Barry Eaton, Dorothée Schneider, Cindy Engel, Marc Bekoff, and many others.

Clarissa v. Reinhardt is the co-author of the books *Stress in Dogs* and *Calming Signals Workbook* (with Martina Scholz), both of which have been translated into many languages. She is a popular speaker in Germany and abroad, who makes a strong case for nonviolent and fair treatment of dogs in her speeches and seminars.

She also makes her expertise and knowledge available to the service of animal welfare. Since 2000, she has run the animal welfare organization, *Houses of Hope,* which cares for dogs, cats, and horses in need. She has developed new concepts for housing dogs in animal shelters and in finding them new homes.

BEHAVIOR & TRAINING

ABC's of Behavior Shaping. Proactive Behavior Mgmt, DVD set. Ted Turner

Aggression In Dogs. Practical Mgmt, Prevention, & Behaviour Modification. Brenda Aloff

Am I Safe? DVD. Sarah Kalnajs

Barking. The Sound of a Language. Turid Rugaas

Behavior Problems in Dogs, 3rd ed. William Campbell

Brenda Aloff's Fundamentals: Foundation Training for Every Dog, DVD. Brenda Aloff

Bringing Light to Shadow. A Dog Trainer's Diary. Pam Dennison

Canine Body Language. A Photographic Guide to the Native Language of Dogs. Brenda Aloff

Changing People Changing Dogs. Positive Solutions for Difficult Dogs. Rev. Dee Ganley

Chill Out Fido! How to Calm Your Dog. Nan Arthur

Clicked Retriever. Lana Mitchell

Dog Behavior Problems. The Counselor's Handbook. William Campbell

Dog Friendly Gardens, Garden Friendly Dogs. Cheryl Smith

Dog Language, An Encyclopedia of Canine Behavior. Roger Abrantes

Dogs are from Neptune. Jean Donaldson

Evolution of Canine Social Behavior, 2nd ed. Roger Abrantes

From Hoofbeats to Dogsteps. A Life of Listening to and Learning from Animals. Rachel Page Elliott

Get Connected With Your Dog, book with DVD. Brenda Aloff

Give Them a Scalpel and They Will Dissect a Kiss, DVD. Ian Dunbar

Guide to Professional Dog Walking And Home Boarding. Dianne Eibner

Language of Dogs, DVD. Sarah Kalnajs

Mastering Variable Surface Tracking, Component Tracking (2 bk set). Ed Presnall

My Dog Pulls. What Do I Do? Turid Rugaas

New Knowledge of Dog Behavior (reprint). Clarence Pfaffenberger

Oh Behave! Dogs from Pavlov to Premack to Pinker. Jean Donaldson

On Talking Terms with Dogs. Calming Signals, 2nd edition. Turid Rugaas

On Talking Terms with Dogs. What Your Dog Tells You, DVD. Turid Rugaas

Play With Your Dog. Pat Miller

Positive Perspectives. Love Your Dog, Train Your Dog. Pat Miller

Positive Perspectives 2. Know Your Dog, Train Your Dog. Pat Miller

Predation and Family Dogs, DVD. Jean Donaldson

Really Reliable Recall. Train Your Dog to Come When Called, DVD. Leslie Nelson

Right on Target. Taking Dog Training to a New Level. Mandy Book & Cheryl Smith

Stress in Dogs. Martina Scholz & Clarissa von Reinhardt

Tales of Two Species. Essays on Loving and Living With Dogs. Patricia McConnell
The Dog Trainer's Resource. The APDT Chronicle of the Dog Collection. Mychelle Blake (*ed*)
The Dog Trainer's Resource 2. The APDT Chronicle of the Dog Collection. Mychelle Blake (*ed*)
The Thinking Dog. Crossover to Clicker Training. Gail Fisher
Therapy Dogs. Training Your Dog To Reach Others. Kathy Diamond Davis
Training Dogs. A Manual (reprint). Konrad Most
Training the Disaster Search Dog. Shirley Hammond
Try Tracking. The Puppy Tracking Primer. Carolyn Krause
Visiting the Dog Park, Having Fun, and Staying Safe. Cheryl S. Smith
When Pigs Fly. Train Your Impossible Dog. Jane Killion
Winning Team. A Guidebook for Junior Showmanship. Gail Haynes
Working Dogs (reprint). Elliot Humphrey & Lucien Warner

HEALTH & ANATOMY, SHOWING
An Eye for a Dog. Illustrated Guide to Judging Purebred Dogs. Robert Cole
Annie On Dogs! Ann Rogers Clark
Another Piece of the Puzzle. Pat Hastings
Canine Cineradiography DVD. Rachel Page Elliott
Canine Massage. A Complete Reference Manual. Jean-Pierre Hourdebaigt
Canine Terminology (reprint). Harold Spira
Breeders Professional Secrets. Ethical Breeding Practices. Sylvia Smart
Dog In Action (reprint). Macdowell Lyon
Dog Show Judging. The Good, the Bad, and the Ugly. Chris Walkowicz
Dogsteps DVD. Rachel Page Elliott
The Healthy Way to Stretch Your Dog. A Physical Theraphy Approach. Sasha Foster and Ashley Foster
The History and Management of the Mastiff. Elizabeth Baxter & Pat Hoffman
Performance Dog Nutrition. Optimize Performance With Nutrition. Jocelynn Jacobs
Positive Training for Show Dogs. Building a Relationship for Success Vicki Ronchette
Puppy Intensive Care. A Breeder's Guide To Care Of Newborn Puppies. Myra Savant Harris
Raw Dog Food. Make It Easy for You and Your Dog. Carina MacDonald
Raw Meaty Bones. Tom Lonsdale
Shock to the System. The Facts About Animal Vaccination... Catherine O'Driscoll
Tricks of the Trade. From Best of Intentions to Best in Show, Rev. Ed. Pat Hastings
Work Wonders. Feed Your Dog Raw Meaty Bones. Tom Lonsdale
Whelping Healthy Puppies, DVD. Sylvia Smart

Dogwise.com is your complete source for dog books on the web!

2,000+ titles, fast shipping, and excellent customer service.

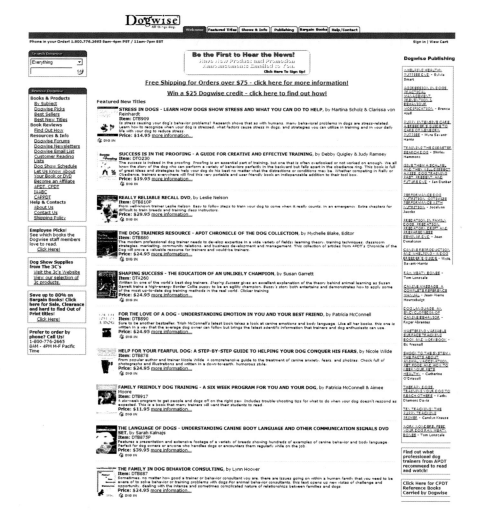